The First Days Of The Internet

The First Days Of The Internet

Internet

punk, art and the world wide web

Ivan Pope

PP
PSYCHAGOGIC
PRESS

The Psychagogic Press

First published by in the UK in 2022 by The Psychagogic Press

www.psychagogic.press

A CIP catalogue record for this book is available from the British Library

ISBN 978-1-7397726-0-4

For my first editor, Marius Pope 1920-2009

And for my buddies, Larry Rees and Richard Ross,
sadly missed.

Look out honey, 'cause I'm using technology
Ain't got time to make no apology

IGGY POP / JAMES WILLIAMSON

SEARCH AND DESTROY

CONTENTS

CONTENTS

It's the Internet, stupid

This book has taken almost twenty years to produce. That's probably a good thing, time gives some perspective and we are now a long, long way away from those mad heady days of 2000 where it ends.

The events that it describes are part of a history that is in danger of being forgotten. It seems impossible now that an art student in London could produce a magazine about the Internet when there were fewer than 100 web sites in the whole world. It seems impossible to have invented the Cybercafe, both the word and the reality. It seems impossible to have started a web production company when nobody knew how to produce web sites. But we did all of this. Every revolution looks impossible after the events just as every revolution eats its own.

I did start writing this book soon after the events described herein but my agent hated it and I gave up for a long time. While researching it I came across a sort of archaeological relic of the original. It's a blog that is still running but to which I no longer have access.

https://ivanpope.wordpress.com/2004/04/21/story-of-web-media/

Ivan Pope/2022

Everybody Wants to Bum A Ride

1976

Elizabeth II, Queen of the United Kingdom sends out an email on 26 March from the Royal Signals and Radar Establishment (RSRE) in Malvern

UUCP (Unix-to-Unix CoPy) developed at AT&T Bell Labs and distributed with UNIX one year later. Multiprocessing Pluribus IMPs are deployed

THEORYNET created by Larry Landweber at Univ of Wisconsin providing electronic mail to over 100 researchers in computer science (using a locally developed email system over TELENET)

RFC 733: Mail specification

First demonstration of ARPANET/SF Bay Packet Radio Net/Atlantic SATNET operation of Internet protocols with BBN supplied gateways in July

[HOBBES' INTERNET TIMELINE]

In the summer of 1976, I went to see David Bowie and the Rolling Stones and dreamt of a world that had gone but which was everywhere present, that I couldn't quite get my head around. I knew something had passed and I longed to be back there, but I also knew it wasn't possible. I had to find my own world.

The second half of the nineteen seventies was a harsh time in England. The joy of the hippies had dissipated and been replaced by political turmoil. Britain had finally joined the European Economic Community. Industrial relations where the same as they ever were. British Leyland workers were on strike at Longbridge. The National Front, a racist political party, marched in London. In October undertakers went on strike and bodies remained unburied.

These things seemed to hover at the edge of my consciousness. They were in the world but not my world. I had access to books, all the books I wanted, to the library and to newspapers. My parents would buy me subscriptions to magazines. For years I had got World of Wonder every week, and I loved that magazine with its articles and pictures about the world. All these things were my proto internet, my coming to understand that the world of information was infinite but could be accessed through portals, that one only had to find these portals to take off.

At the start of 1977, during the fallow days after the Christmas holiday, a rumour went around my school that David Bowie would be touring again soon. I'd been to see him the year before, taking my nine-year-old brother to see the Thin White Duke return. For a family of Bowie acolytes, it had been a major event and I was keen to repeat it. Standing in the playground I asked my friend, Jeremy, if he would go to see him this time, but he said there was another band he would much rather see.

'They are called The Sex Pistols,' he told me. At that moment, although I didn't know it, a low door in the wall began to open. After school that day we went down to the local record store where I bought a punk single. It was Grip by The Stranglers and for a long time I thought it was the most beautiful object I would ever own.

I grew up in Royal Tunbridge Wells and went to the local grammar school. I was a classic skinny blond haired English boy who dreamed about the world and found it difficult to keep focused on anything. I knew that I was dead smart but I was bad at being in school. I was good at causing disturbances and in that way my school career was irreparably damaged.. I was full of ideas but didn't know how to behave unless it involved causing trouble and being difficult. I was fascinated by the world but didn't know how to communicate, or who would be interested. My troubles had started long before punk, but punk was what demonstrated to me how to live a certain type of life.

It is hard to know quite what order events occurred in that year, it quickly became a blur. Looking back, I can say with certainty that punk ruined me and punk gave me life. It opened my eyes, made me brave and showed me that anything was possible. I absorbed a message that work was pointless, that you needed to fight, to be an anarchist, that the world had it in for you, that you could do anything you wanted, that it was easy, it was cheap and we should go and do it. I held all this tight to my heart and it set the route map for my life. I may have been like this anyway, but punk makes a convenient scapegoat.

I was fifteen that year, a little too late to be fully involved in this new music scene. Maybe one year older would have made all the difference. I couldn't leave school, though I tried hard, I couldn't get a job, I couldn't leave home, I couldn't move to London. I was mired in my provincial town, close enough to London but not quite close enough. I ended up excluded me from a club that I would like to be a member of the people who made a difference. I always wanted to be a founder of something.

What you really need when you are a teenager is a mad aggressive dangerous challenging loud inspiring pile of noise and attitude that tells you to get up and do something, makes you believe that you can do anything. Did anything like the punk ever come so precisely gauged into a world so ripe for change? Suddenly it was 1977 and this dark, violent, creative scene became own world. Punk was my first epiphany. I experienced it as an immediate realisation, a religious conversion. I just knew. It was my first time, but not my last. Somehow my brain could do that, could find things as revealed. I proceeded by epiphany and what I found took the place of any religion, any organised belief. I was left to find my own sacraments and they came to me in droves.

The first days of my new life were out of focus but seemed to make perfect sense. A dire grey half-decade of strange stasis was ending suddenly. A world that had started in the sixties was violently overthrown. Never trust a hippie, said Johnny Rotten. Everyone had had enough. My generation, born long after the war, moved towards the light.

The year before in the kitchen at home my sister had showed me a newspaper article about kids wearing strange militaristic outfits and Nazi regalia to clubs in London. The newspaper was laughing at them and we laughed too, but we were also attracted by the transgression. We didn't know what we were looking at.

At the end of 1976 the Sex Pistols appeared gurning and swearing on The Ed Grundy Show and the seventies imploded in fear and loathing. The Grundy Show was an ordinary show for ordinary people and they booked a band at the last minute without paying much attention after someone else dropped out. The presenter couldn't resist encouraging this band to swear, so they did, again and again. Someone kicked their television set in and we were made.

The Pistols came out of nowhere and changed everything in one blinding flash, in the time it took for the needle to drop onto the vinyl and the first rolling, frightening, chords of God Save The Queen to emerge. With my precocious teenage imagination, I thought this is what the German invasion of the Soviet Union must have sounded like. I had friends who would spend entire parties, entire nights, playing that single again and again until it wore out.

In the way of major disruptions to the established order, they neither planned nor controlled what happened, and much of what came after was really the remaking of the old order, but this little group, who never sold much and who blew up a few months later, recreated the world in a new image.

I never did see them play. Their tour was fell apart, they fell apart, I was too young, too broke. Some people I knew chased them across the country, and if I'd been a couple of years older I might have done the same, but I wasn't. By the time I began to travel to see bands, they were gone. That much was noted by most observers, certainly by those who were directly affected, and then the impact of those few weeks span outwards and upwards and sucked in huge parts of international life and attitude and all of us eager kids who were waiting to find out what our world was going to consist of.

In the first days there was no language to describe what was happening. Quickly we acquired a language all of our own and put it to work and it was in this that I realised what my role could be. They say Sid Vicious invented the pogo, which basically involved jumping up and down on the spot. There was a process called gobbling, which involved spitting huge amounts of phlegm at the band and covering them from head to toe in foul expectorant. I'm still ashamed of gobbling to this day. Someone came up with the term poser as a form of abuse and it a ached itself to anyone who didn't make the cut, or who was suspected of not quite making the cut in whatever small circle you hung out with. The word punk itself seems to have come from America where it has a very derogatory meaning, but in England it seemed like something that had just been invented. The culture was invented from the ground up. No matter the revisionism, a tiny group of people changed the world using elements from a variety of existing sources. It wasn't a plot and it wasn't a swindle. Human nature being what it is, everyone involved found they had to make it all up as they went along, and they did. We greedily grabbed these new terms, a language with which to set ourselves apart from everything that had come before and everything that wasn't us.

I went to see the Clash play in Hastings, a venue on a pier that stretched out over the sea. The ticket cost less than a pound. I knew the pier well from sea fishing with my brother— now it brought a far more intense pleasure to my life. On the way to the gig, in Boots in the town, I asked to hear the Sex Pistols' single, Anarchy in the UK, but the woman behind the counter took fright and wouldn't pay it. She put it in a bag, handed it to me and asked for 79p. I paid.

The Clash schooled me. Their politics were worn on their sleeve but did not amount to much apart from anthems of rebellion. In many ways their worldview and politics seemed old fashioned, as if they had been formed in an earlier era, which of course they had. When they sang, "I don't mind the stars and stripes, let's print the Watergate tapes ..." they were harking back to something that most punks probably didn't recall, or care about. On their second album, Give 'Em Enough Rope, in 1978 they pointed out on All the Young Punks that while everybody wanted to be famous, they had made the effort, they had gone out and got their name on the poster. Even if you start small, you are making headway. That was my trigger. I got it, although it took a few years to find out what poster I wanted to be on.

The whole thing about gigs, about punk, was the combination of theory and practice, the absolute sublimation of desire into a chosen form. Gigs were about the pinnacle of action, time and vision, a fusion of everything that life seemed to offer with darkness and beer and violence and noise thrown in. What more could anyone want?

The bands were variable. We didn't have any money or any way to travel except by train, so what we got to see was hit and miss. The concerts acted as much as social events, as bonding sessions where we would strut and pose and act up, where we were safe in a crowd. Other times, we were not so safe.

After that first gig I knew I had to see more bands and I started going to London to find them. With my friend, Graham, we formed a tag team, bumping trains to the capital and exploring the geography of punk. Kings Road, Notting Hill, Wardour Street, Covent Garden - where the gigs were, where the shops were, where punks congregated. At weekends you could go and hang out on the Kings Road, ducking in and out of the shops, Sex, Seditionaries, scared of the cool people who ran them but close to the beating heart of something. Something was happening.

Something tugged at me deep inside and, although it was uncomfortable and I had no idea what it really was, I wanted desperately to answer its call. Soon after discovering this new world, I gave up on school. Now what had been a battleground, a fight with everyone, turned into something I just avoided. I was a sliver, I took myself off to town during the long days, hanging out all over the place. I was in love with a skinny girl called Tracey and took to looking for her during school hours. We would go and hang out in a bedsit whose occupants was at work, a friend who let us hang out, smoke and play records in his crummy room and sometimes Tracey and her friend and Graham would all hang out in that room, all day long, broke, hungry, horny, lovelorn and then Graham and his girl would grapple under the covers while I sat frozen, unable to say anything to Tracey. I was still a virgin, I had no idea how to broach the subject of sex with girls, how to find a girlfriend. But I understood the power of music and, more and more, the value of drink and drugs to make up for the void.

Footage and photos from the early days of punk show a culture in transition. Teenagers took what they had to hand and adapted it to become punk and in doing so they adapted themselves to become punk. For a while nobody knew what this thing was which had come out of nowhere with a ferocity. What to do about it? The mannered mohicans, beloved of tourists, didn't exist. Nobody had elaborately studded leather jackets or well chiseled faces, cleansed by amphetamine sulphate and Special Brew. We were seventies kids with no money and no heroes, certainly of the type we craved. It was, however, fairly easy to approximate the look of Johnny Rotten.

It was a mix of dressing up and attitude. Some of those present have picked up on the style and run with it, taking a huge chance on a punk aesthetic. It was all completely homemade. Some have stuck a toe in the water, writing on their jackets, donning a dog's collar, wearing lurid makeup, pinning swastikas to their clothes. When I went to my first punk gig the people I travelled down with tore gaping holes in their flares on the train. They were music fans, they were doing what they had always done, going to see a new band. Something in the air told them that they had to fit in, to make an effort. They started to shred their nice respectable flares and sweaters. They left town as local boys and arrived at the coast as punk rockers.

The person who names the new thing can own up owning it and I guess I learnt some lessons from watching punk develop. I was too young and too detached to name anything for punk. The big boys came up with the words, but we all transitioned that year and we were never going back.

There was of course more to punk than aggression, the Sex Pistols and loud music. The true core of the movement came quietly behind this theatre of rolling thunder. Ideas like boredom, urban ennui and unemployability surfaced. My desire for stimulation, the need to find new things, emerged. I knew I'd never be in a band - I couldn't sing and didn't have the focus to learn to play an instrument - but what I could do was write, what I did understand was how to make a publication.

For Christmas my parents bought me a proper camera, a heavy metal and chrome single lens reflex job and before long I was jumping up on stage and chasing bands back into the dressing room after gigs as well as writing the copy for a new version of the zine. Before long I was selling it in London, at Rough Trade. I had made my first breakthrough into a strange combination of creativity and writing and publishing and commercial attitude that was to repeat itself in various forms. I still had no idea what I was doing, but I found I knew how to do it.

I wanted to emulate something that touched me. This was my thing; I was up and running. I wanted to write and create and publish and I had my subject. I found that there were more people around who wanted to write and make a magazine, so I soon become an editor and a publisher. My friends and I made a fanzine between us. We interviewed bands. We would meet them at gigs, jump on the stage afterwards and follow them into the dressing room. We also nicked a load of stuff and I made up a lot of nonsense, but this was real. I was shit scared of everyone, shy as anything as always, but I did it because there was no alternative.

A richer friend gave me ten pounds get the zine photocopied, my first brush with angel funding — I still respect that offer, it taught me that there were many ways of being involved in a project. It also taught me about funding. I got a hundred copies photocopied in the high street. The local record shop sold them and I took some up to Rough Trade, which was the punk record shop in Notting Hill, London, because that's what I'd read you do with fanzines. They took some and sold the lot.

The railway to London presented an opportunity and a challenge. We never had any money, or what little we had could not be wasted on the fare to London, three or four pounds, so bumping the trains became our acquired habit.

The railways were less fenced and less guarded with no technology to hold us back, but there were ticket collectors at every entrance with a human insistence on actually seeing a ticket. There were ways around this human barrier but which one to use depended on luck, circumstance and chance. There was also the ever-present danger of the ticket inspector on the train. For this one could hide in the toilet, the trick being to not lock the door and hope the inspector passed by without giving it a shove. You could stand on the toilet bowl to avert this danger, letting the door fly open and closed again. Other tricks involved keeping ahead of the inspector as he moved down the train and waiting for an opportunity to slip past him while he was diverted.

The trains themselves were slam door diesels, well past their prime but part of the great commuter stock of the South East. My father would climb on board one every morning along with a motley crew of lawyers, stockbrokers, accountants and other Tunbridge Wells men. He did this without fail for almost twenty years, which seemed a lot longer while he was commuting.

It wasn't only young punks who bumped the trains. Our neighbour, a respectable lawyer and pillar of the community, was watched as he used a first-class carriage repeatedly while holding a second-class season ticket. Eventually the inspectors pounced and he was taken to court and humiliated. I also suffered prosecution for my nefarious railway activities. I had discovered a fine exit route from the station when returning to Tunbridge Wells from London. There was a huge goods lift at the end of the platform which could be summoned with a button. It was unguarded and provided a good way to escape the terrors of the ticket barrier. One morning, returning from a night spent on Euston Station, I took my usual route. When the door opened at the top of the shaft a British Rail man stood waiting for me, eager to spring the trap.

I was summonsed to the magistrate's court and given a fine of sixty pounds, a huge sum at a time when the monthly dole was thirteen pounds, and something I had no chance of ever paying.

The injustice of that huge punishing fine on a penniless boy still rankles.

We knew how we wanted to dress but there was nowhere to buy our clothes except in the Kings Road and we didn't have any money. The music mags were still full of adverts for army coats and sheepskin jackets, the hippy economy was in full swing. The shops on the Kings Road were far too expensive for us, but we liked to go and hang out in them at weekends. We got most of our clothes from jumble sales, buying old shirts and suits and them chopping them up and decorating them at home. I found that I enjoyed inventing techniques for altering clothes, possibly my first pure creative work.

I cut my hair off, creating a short spiky mess which didn't suit my face. I didn't really have a punk face, but then nobody did. If you look at photos of early gigs you just see a bunch of kids wearing whatever they had put on in the morning. It was only later that the punk look became associated with studded jackets and Mohican haircuts, by which time the whole thing was over, had become a cartoon version of itself.

Just being dressed as a punk carried its own dangers, especially when you weren't in a group and we were assailed and thumped on many occasions. We took it all as part of the life and were inspired by the Clash singing, *Though we get beat up, we don't care, at least it livens up the air.*[2] We hung out in the punk clothing shops Sex, Seditionaries and Boy, though we could never afford to buy anything. We lusted after the bondage trousers, but on the whole we looked then went home and copied them in our own way. Weekends were a theatre of confrontation with gangs of revivalist Teddy Boys who would march up from the Worlds End end of the Kings Road. We would gather in Sloane Square and running battles would ensure with the press in attendance. When we ventured down the road there was always the danger of being caught by the older and bigger Teds. One day we got chased back up and my friend ducked into a food shop, picking up cans of beans to pelt anyone who followed him in with.

One day in Boy, a mecca for out of towners, we met a woman trying on bondage trousers. We started talking to her. She turned out to be the actress, Candy Clarke, who had played Mary-Lou in Nick Roeg's David Bowie movie, The Man Who Fell to Earth, the previous year. To us she seemed very old and sophisticated, though she was barely thirty at the time. She was in England making The Big Sleep for Michael Winner. We hadn't really shaken Bowie out of our systems and to meet an American film star from a film like that was a dream. We talked to her about punk and what was going on around town. She was intrigued by the whole thing and bought a pair of trousers, spending about £33, a huge sum to us. Then she took us across the road to a pub and bought us drinks.

We spent a lot of time trying to get into gigs without paying. In July The Clash played four nights at the Music Machine in Camden and I bumped the trains up for one of the gigs without any money or ticket. I sat in the pub opposite with my single drink, enjoying the atmosphere but wishing I could get in. Out of nowhere my sister turned up in a great mood and told me she had a way in. She'd met a guy. He took us round the back of the venue and we climbed up onto a garage roof, then higher up fire escapes, up and up until we emerged onto the roof. The place had a huge copper dome on the roof and I was staggered to find that we were suddenly standing next to it. This guy reached down and lifted up a hatch and we scrambled down a ladder inside. Then he took us quietly down a couple of corridors until we stood by a door. 'One by one', he said, 'quickly'. He pulled the door open and I slipped through, finding myself on one of the upper levels of the music hall style venue. I looked down at the crowd, the place was rocking. It was about the most exciting entrance I'd ever made to a gig although I'd seen the Clash quite a few times by then. Punk had come a long way and a lot of variants were emerging, but the Clash were obviously supreme in a combination of the combination of songwriting and performance. Every Clash gig was a dream and they just got better and better. Charles Shaar-Murray, reviewing the gig for the NME, said simply 'this is the heyday of The Clash.'

There was a support band from New York for these gigs, a strange band called Suicide. They were very much part of the New York punk scene and had invented a whole sound of their own using primitive synthesisers and vocals. Unfortunately, the punk scene in England was becoming insular. The music was changing from experimental strangeness to the reproduction of what the crowds came to hear. So, while everyone loved the Clash (even then, there were repeated calls for White Riot from their first album, which the band refused to play), they had problems with Suicide. As they played their strange New York synthesiser drone a hail of bottles flew onto the stage. They just kept on playing. They'd seen a lot worse over the years. I was transfixed, I thought they were amazing and told myself I would get their album as soon as I could. I became addicted to their first album and would play it again and again along with Throbbing Gristle. The track Frankie Teardrop, with its screaming ending, was always a favourite.

Many years later, in the nineties, I met them at the afterparty following a gig in the Holloway Road. My brother had taken the publicity photos for them, The Return of the 21 and got me an invite to the after party upstairs. I waited in the dark bar for what seemed like an age. Eventually Martin Rev emerged and sat on his own.

I went over an sat down and told him I'd loved the gig that night. 'I saw you support the Clash at the Music Machine,' I said. He laughed. 'That was a harsh gig,'

My dad told me they wanted an article from a punk for his paper. I'd been up to the Kings Road that weekend where confrontations with Teddy Boys had drawn press attention and we'd run up and down the street and caused a ruckus, although really nothing had happened. I wrote about it, criticising the newspapers for making things up and name checking the punk shops, Sex and Seditionaries. For the article I went to London and had my photo taken round the corner from the Evening Standard offices. I sat in the park and a fat photographer took my picture. I didn't know what was going on. They published what I wrote and sent me a cheque after a few months. I was a published writer and I'd been paid for it. But it meant nothing to me, it didn't occur to me to try and get more work published. I wasn't confident at all and I was very angry about nothing in particular.

My sister, who had grown into a big brave protective gregarious beauty, got herself arrested on the Kings Road. The arrest was captured on film as Janet Street Porter, a big toothed working class self-promoting member of the existing media elite, was making a documentary, The Year of Punk, for London Weekend Television. Hanging out in the Kings Road, Chelsea, she interviewed a motley collection of kids who wear a variety of outfits, some bordering on the ludicrous. The video still exists on the internet. The punks are nothing like what they will become, there are no leather jackets, no mohicans, not even any bondage trousers. Most people were so new to the idea of punk that they hadn't yet started wearing punk gear, it hardly existed outside expensive boutiques like Sex and Seditionaries. Street-Porter is creating the spectacle and she knows it. It is clear that punk is an attractive proposition.

My parents got a call from the Chelsea police station and my dad set off, with me as company, to bail her out. It was nothing that a bit of middle-class bonhomie couldn't sort out, and my father wasn't cross, though he may have been mortified. On the way we stopped and called my mother back at home. She told us that Capital Radio wanted to interview me, following my article. I guess my dad liked the idea of his son getting some media attention. It was, after all, his life. We drove to the radio station and I was interviewed about my punk life. I can't remember anything about my interview, but I have total recall of the moment that the interviewer turned to my father. 'What do you make of all this, Mr Pope?' he asked. My father seized the moment. 'Well, it's all fairly familiar to me. I can remember when I was young and my mother wouldn't let me have a corduroy jacket.' It was both funny and mortifying and I realised that my father harboured some teenage grudges of his own.

I came to relish the opportunity to go out with her, she had a peerless eye for trouble, she adopted waifs and strays on the street and an evening in her company inevitably ended in high drama or the experience of a lifetime. At the same time, as a shy introvert I was often mortified by her interaction with strangers, her questions to passers-by. It was a matter of taking the rough with the smooth, but all in all you couldn't wish for a better big sister.

After I'd run away from home and been brought back, I was introduced to amphetamines in the pub by some friends. Here, have this blue pill, they said, and I knew a low door was opening again. I would have taken anything at that point, I think most of us would, we knew drugs existed and smoked dope a lot, but bigger harder drugs were what we craved.

We wanted to be grown up.

The pill that first night was a bluey, a tablet of speed. There were blues and there were yellows for a short while, the yellows were Dexedrine from which came the band, Dexies Midnight Runners. We were at the end of an era of these sorts of drugs: they soon disappeared and I seldom saw them again. But on that first night I was given or bought a blue pill and we all took them and then got a taxi back up to someone's flat where those who knew what to expect settled in for a long night of mad chat. I fell for speed.

The version that I loved, amphetamine sulphate, a white powder, came later. After a while everyone gave it up because it was a difficult and dangerous game. Those who gave it up smoked huge amounts of hash and those who didn't graduated to harder pleasures such as heroin, but I enjoyed the simple pleasure of amphetamine, it was my bag. It was best on hot summer days when it would lift your spirits and your feet so that you could walk down the road taking enormous strides, as if you had eight league boots on. It was a disgusting drug to taste, if you snorted it you would be sniffing the residue down into your throat for hours, each time getting a sharp astringent hit which was both revolting and wonderful. Others took to swallowing small wraps of it in cigarette papers so it went directly into your digestion. But it remained a hard to obtain drug, rare and beautiful and I loved it. For a while it was rumoured to be produced in the Gillette research lab in Reading where my cousin lived and I told everyone that was where it came from.

After punk started to fizzle out I gave up on school. I left because I just didn't see what the point of it was in school and the school didn't see what the point was in me. If you weren't sporty or heading for Oxbridge, if you were difficult they hardly made any effort to keep you on. School leaving age was sixteen, it had only recently been raised from fifteen, and you could go off and get a job the moment you were that age. I had been bunking off since before punk started, not going to school, hanging around in town. I spent endless hours in the library, reading the papers and then rooting through the provincial collection of books. I would spend entire days in the reference library or in the museum next door, or in the old swimming pool that now had tennis table tables available for hire. I was in love with a girl called Tracy who didn't care much for me and I longed to meet her in town. Sometimes I did. For an entire winter we hid in the bedsit of someone we vaguely knew, listening to records and eating biscuits, sometimes snogging or making out.

I had a yearning in my heart, a desire so strong to do something. I left school early. My mum sent me to stay with her sister in Abingdon, to revise. I rode there on my motorbike, a Honda CB175, which I loved dearly, but found life in this even smaller town more boring than being at home. I went back to school to take my exams, and passed six of them, but I was beyond caring about education, I didn't understand what the point was. University was held out as an opportunity, but nobody really seemed to know why. As neither of my parents had been it wasn't really as if they could explain how it had helped them.

I went to the college in the next town, riding there on my motorbike and doing next to no work. A levels, English, Economics and something. After a few months I heard about a journalism course and transferred to that, but couldn't stick learning to type, learning shorthand. I had tasted revolution and didn't want to settle back. I smoked a lot of dope and drank when I could, now not raging against the system but utterly futilely bored.

Punk had a cartoonish attitude to employment and it had a lasting impact. I've barely ever had a real job, one that wasn't invented by me for me. This made perfect sense in those times with the ending of an erstwhile socialist state having into view, it also impacted a generation. It gave us an internalised view that work was something to be avoided, that there were other routes through life that were more valid. And even if there were jobs, there were no careers and it was better to avoid that whole soulless nine to five and remain a punk. It took me decades to realise that attention deficit causes lack of career development. An inability to retain interest in work, to always be seeking some new stimulation, tended to cause a lack of interest in jobs in the first place and then a tendency to walk out or to leave on a whim when you did get one.

I didn't have the dedication to remain a punk, my attention had wondered. I needed something new to distract me. All the same, somehow the meme of punk, the essential rejectionist theory, got under my skin and put me in a very difficult position. It probably would have happened anyway, my undiagnosed attention deficit disorder made me a prime candidate for shirking, for refusing to work, for carrying a sense of desire for something else, but punk didn't help. There was an otherness to me that I had no idea how to explain or use but I knew that music and rebellion and soon drugs and alcohol added up to something. I just didn't know what.

Then Sid killed Nancy and everything changed.

The streets filled with tourist bait wearing studded leather jackets and mohicans. The bands became more crude, violent, skinheads became fascist, there was fighting everywhere. And the Clash went off to be stadium stars in America.

I could never have lasted, except in the hearts and minds of a generation who had absorbed the lessons of punk and were never going to give it up. It would take a couple of decades for this attitude to come to power.

I internalised some stupid lessons which served me badly. There are no jobs, at least, none that you might want. *Do you wanna make tea at the BBC, do you wanna be, do you really wanna be a cop?* I refused to work; I couldn't see how it was possible. I did get a job at a builders' merchants in the next town and I rode over there every day on my motorbike and I loved it for a while before I went away. But after that, I was done with the job thing. Punk made me like that. Punk and attention deficit.

The eighties arrived along with yuppies, Princess Diana and New Romantics, a lot of soft, squishy, music, affluence and pretty people. Punk's not dead, they shouted, but it was in most ways that mattered.

Punk lasted about five minutes. To a teenager that five minutes could sustain you for decades. The Mohican's and leather jackets, the hard-core bands, the posing for tourists, the violence and hard drugs, that all came later. It was a spasm of rebellion with some great music, a chance to go and see bands, to be in a big gang, to make a magazine. I had learnt to be a photographer, to get on stage and dive into the changing room, to interview bands, to do what I wanted to do. I wore clothes that I made myself. We went to the Kings Road but could never afford to buy anything. With a sewing machine we worked out the essential message of punk: you can do it yourself. Or, as the Desperate Bicycles sang, it was easy, it was cheap, go and do it.

What I learnt from punk was how music can be a code for being in a gang and being in a gang can be code for what you believe in and what you believe in can be invented for yourself. No need any longer to take it from anyone else, I was now out on my own with a life to create.

Nothing was going to be the same again after that, we were free, though it was going to take a lot longer than would seem possible to understand what it all meant.

With 1977 came not only punk but soon reggae as well. Jamaican band Culture released an album called Two Sevens Clash, a response to the prophecy that when the two sevens came together things would happen in the world. It was a beautiful and heartbreaking record to me, a record to fall in love with and to fall in love to.

My punky gang grew bigger. I had never known anything like it, I was a part of something bigger than me and when I went out my clothes, my attitude, they gave me an identity and a belonging. I was in a gang and I met and recognised other gangs. We were all on the same side, all wearing the same things and all in the same secret adventure. People were scared of us. We were scared of ourselves but the truth was that something was exploding all around us and we wanted so much to be in on it.

In 1979 my father and the rest of my family went back to South Africa to visit our cousins. They had come across the world several times, flush with the high value of the Rand, and had livened up our lives with outings, presents, strange language and cash gifts. My first experience of grass came from my cousin Jackie, a mild South African hippy.

In the political field nuclear disarmament and anti-racism sat alongside anti-apartheid campaigning and I generally boycotted events that involved my apartheid family, despite loving them dearly. Following a visit, my father wrote about going back after twenty years. He didn't mean it to be an apologia for apartheid, but the newspaper wanted people to read it that way.

The end of the seventies brought Margaret Thatcher almost as a punishment for punk. The movement, such as it was, grew out of a socialist Labour world where work was the main point of life. By the time punk was drawing to the end of its swift and miraculous life the Labour world was ending, although none of us knew it for a while.

I was sent to Israel, to a kibbutz, as a tribute to my father's forebears and to the reality of the situation - that I really wasn't about to do anything else. I got there just after the election of the first Thatcher government, something to which I hadn't given much thought.

2

London Calling

1988

Internet worm burrows through the Net, affecting ~6,000 of the 60,000 hosts on the Internet (:ph1:) CERT (Computer Emergency Response Team) formed by DARPA in response to the needs exhibited during the Morris worm incident. The worm is the only advisory issued this year.

Internet Assigned Numbers Authority (IANA) established in December with Jon Postel as its Director. Postel was also the RFC Editor and US Domain registrar for many years.

Internet Relay Chat (IRC) developed by Jarkko Oikarinen (:zby:)

First Canadian regionals join NSFNET: ONet via Cornell, RISQ via Princeton, BCnet via Univ of Washington (:ec1:) FidoNet gets connected to the Net, enabling the exchange of email and news (:tp1:)

The first multicast tunnel is established between Stanford and BBN in the Summer of 1988.

Countries connecting to NSFNET: Canada (CA), Denmark (DK), France (FR), Iceland (IS), Norway (NO), Sweden (SE)

[HOBBES' INTERNET TIMELINE]

In the mid-eighties after years drifting in Europe and losing my way and my mind in my hometown I finally did what I should have done long before—moved to London. It was inevitable—it had been my second home since my sister had moved to the Isle of Dogs in the late seventies—but it took me a long time to find a way to actually make the move. In the end it was more of an absorption, a gathering in. The city was part of my DNA, so close it was inevitable I would end up there, and it happened without me really thinking about it.

Two girls I'd met while hanging out in Crete, Jo and Jenny, were now living in Crouch End, in short life housing. She explained how their house was managed by a co-op. In the early eighties, when squatting had started to get out of hand, councils has struck a bargain. The squatters could become licensed on a short-term basis. They would pay rates but no rent, and would undertake some repairs on the buildings to keep them livable in. Their occupancy would keep real squatters and vandals out and, when the buildings were needed, the occupants would move on. Short life housing was born and it flourished, managed by rackety co-operative setups. Short life housing allowed the councils to keep tabs on their property and to, in theory, get them back when they were required.

They invited me to move up and stay with them until the co-op reopened its doors to new members. Then I'd be able to join and get my own property. They were working as cycle couriers, well settled back in London and earning a fair amount of money. Jo's dad ran a record stall on Brick Lane market where I'd always bought albums. I moved into a tiny spare room they had on the landing below the kitchen. I moved a bed, a record player and various bits of furniture in and settled in quickly. I signed on for unemployment benefit and started looking around London for interesting things to do. The flat was decent but hacked around a bit and painted in lurid colours. They had built a kitchen on the landing and next to it was a bathroom which seemed to have been carved into the roof space. A huge cast iron roll top bath was a luxury, but the bath was not fixed to the floor and could become a terrible liability if one tried to climb out without taking extreme care. My girlfriend was at university in Sheffield but came down regularly for visits when we huddled in my freezing room, but Jo and Jenny looked after me as I worked on converting myself into a Londoner.

Although I knew London fairly well, certainly well enough not to be scared of it, it still seemed like I had moved to another planet. And that was a good thing. For the first year of my new life, I cut myself off fairly comprehensively from my previous one. I didn't visit my old friends.

There were no Google maps then. We relied on the A-Z of London; a book of maps that had been created by a somewhat visionary but slightly fraudulent woman after the war. When you move to a new city you don't look at it, you don't see it. You don't know what has changed, what is changing, what you could have seen, what is new. You just see what you need to see. I saw a city that was available and that quickly absorbed me. I didn't see the struggle that the city was engaged in, the past or the future. Only at the end of my time in that metropolis, and now, do I wonder what I missed at that time and how it was different.

Of course, I didn't know I was remapping myself, that knowledge could only come with hindsight, once the process had finished, but I had embarked without knowing it on conversion into an artist. This was something that I could never have done back home. In my hometown everyone knew me and my family and my past. In London I was nobody and that was the best place to start again.

The town I had moved to was very different to the one my parents had left twenty years before, but also, in many ways, much the same. The bad times of the seventies were becoming a distant memory, Thatcherism was starting to bite — or open up new opportunities, depending on who you were and what you wanted to do. I retained my leftist anarchic worldview; I didn't want anything to do with Thatcher or her works. On the other hand, it was almost impossible to avoid getting drawn into the potential that the market economy held out. I had no issues at all with being a capitalist, so long as I could be a nice sort of capitalist and do what I wanted to do. Of course, none of this was articulated that winter.

Jo and Jenny were the best hosts I could have had. They continued as dispatch riders, suffering with the winter weather but earning decent money. The government gave me a pretend job with a pretend agency called MACMA, the Mutual Aid Management Company. The government had set up various schemes to massage the employment figures and this was one of them. They gave me a job working in one of their offices in a shop front on the Lower Clapton Road, just north of a very ungentrified Hackney. Supervised by an unemployed Welshman, who seemed to me to be an old man but who was probably about forty, I read the papers and made a collection of cuttings. I have little idea of what I was supposed to be doing, but I told everyone that I had my perfect job — reading the papers every day. I sent out a lot of letters, but to whom I have no idea.

One evening in the spring of 1996 Jo came home excited and told me that the housing coop was finally ready to re-open its doors and admit new members.

'They have enough housing for a new set of members, but it's going to be very competitive,' she said. 'You need to get down there immediately and queue up.' It was Friday afternoon and the office wouldn't open until Monday morning.

'Are you totally crazy?' I said, but she was adamant.

'Get down there now and get a place in the queue,' she said. 'I'll bring you some things down later.'

Grudgingly I caught the bus down to the Habberfield office in a grotty shopfront. To my amazement there were already people lined up outside. I joined them on the pavement. Soon the queue stretched down the street and we allocated ourselves numbers to mark our places. Good as her word, Jo turned up on her bike with soup and bread and my sleeping bag.

'You're going to be here all weekend,' she said.

I had already started to get to know the people around me and as the night wore on we bonded in adversity. Two more friends from Crete turned up, also eager for accommodation.

The queue turned into a party. The nights were warm and beer was fetched from nearby shops and shared around. We quickly got to know each other. It may have become somewhat rowdy and I'm sure I was loud mouthed, although I remember it as a time of laughter and good humour. Near the front of the queue, better organised than me, was a woman from Norfolk called Carol. She had moved to the city to join her boyfriend, Steve, who, like me, was already living in Habberfield short life housing. Steve was a beautiful and strange boy, like a goth crossed with a spaceman and Carol was feisty and scary to me, but also friendly and generous. As we got to know each other during that weekend they got the impression that I was a loudmouthed fool and Steve later admited telling Carol, 'I never want to share a house with that guy.'

A few months later I moved in with them to their huge but cold flat on Lordship Lane, right opposite Broadwater Farm where riots had occurred the previous year and led to the death of PC Blakemore.

Settled in London, I started to think about what I wanted to do. I didn't really have much idea, but I came up with an idea for a book. I'd given up smoking quickly and successfully, and I decided to write a book to help others do the same, structured as a diary. Although I could use the public libraries, I was more ambitious and so I applied for a readers pass at the British Library, which at that time was still ensconced in the middle of British Museum, right in the centre of London. I had to explain in some detail why I needed a pass, which I did. I knew I was interested in finding out a lot of facts to go in my Anti-Smoking Diary and I wanted to research the history of tobacco and smoking. They gave me a pass and I entered the hallowed halls of the library that Lenin had used. It was an archaic and old-fashioned establishment which you entered via the museum. The decor was classic British institutional, lots of tiling and exposed pipes in the corridors on the way in. Once in the place you could doze all day at the huge wooden desks while waiting for books to be brought to you. I loved the exclusiveness of it, the feeling that I was privileged, that I was allowed to come in here and hide away from the world.

I wrote up a proposal for my book and sent it off to one publisher. I chose Virgin books as they seemed to be producing slightly off-centre books that had a sort of zeitgeist feel to them. I would go to the Virgin megastore on Oxford street and look at everything that was being published and get inspired. I'm sure my proposal was amateurish, even if my idea still strikes me as quite good. After a while I got a nice letter back saying that while they liked my idea they couldn't see how my book would fit in with their subjects.

Rather than being disheartened, I was excited. Richard Branson was still something of a hero and Virgin retained some vestige of being a trendy company. As far as I could see, a real publisher had replied to me, and they weren't being rude or dismissive. The book went nowhere but the idea of coming up with commercial ideas stuck with me.

In Crete I had dabbled in making jewellery out of various objects, collecting stones and shells and assembling findings to add to them. These attempts to make and sell jewellery ended in failure, but I remained interested in the idea. My interest was sparked by my sister who turned up one day with bangles made from bent and twisted cutlery which she had picked up in the Petticoat Lane market. I bought some forks and tried to emulate these but it seemed impossible. In Tunbridge Wells I made some passable pieces out of beads and wire and even sold a few. Then I took silver-smithing lessons at the local Adult Education Centre and learnt to make silver objects. My dad was, as always ahead of me with a love of tools worked, had got into model engineering and model shipbuilding. He bought me a beautiful soldering torch that ran on butane. He loved making things, though he could never stay with any hobby.

My mother tolerated his expensive interests and laughed at the number of things he'd been interested in since she had met him. It took me years to understand that I was exactly the same as him, that I had the same ability to fall deeply in love with a subject and to acquire tools or knowledge to undertake it, only to fall suddenly out of love with the same subject. The combination of desire to be hands on and make objects combined with the ability to come up with great ideas, to understand the world and how to bring new things into it — that was my dad and that was me. The pattern of my life was set even before I was born. Years later he would end up doing silver-smithing himself, at the same adult education centre, and making my children beautiful silver objects that they still have.

I was reading about craft jewellers and became hooked on these incredible handmade objects. My aunt, who was a po er and who noticed my interest, bought me a subscription to Crafts magazine as a birthday present and a whole new world opened up for me. In I had access to an array of galleries and exhibitions to visit enthusiastically — they were free entertainment and I was almost constantly broke. When I got home I would make my own jewellery and design insane objects, drawing and sticking into my notebooks with love but little idea of what I was doing. I hadn't connected the assemblages I had been making for most of my life with this new obsession, but I was getting closer.

Sitting in my cold little room in Harvey Road off Crouch End, I decided I would go to college and learn to make jewellery properly. I'd never had an art lesson in my life, at school they'd made me do woodwork and then engineering drawing, but I started drawing again in my own time so I'd have some stuff to show. I asked Haringey council about it. They said if I wanted to go to art college I had to do a Foundation course first, then I might get onto a three-dimensional design degree course. They told me that as there weren't any Foundation courses in the borough, so I could choose between the Middlesex Poly course at Cat Hill or one of the central London colleges such as St Martins or Central School of Art. I had no idea what any of these were so I applied to Cat Hill out on the fringes of London. Cat Hill was in Barnet, a place that had become a Jewish suburb populated by a generation of Jews who moved out and up from Hackney, having originated in that primal immigrant soup around Brick Lane in Whitechapel. My London experience was shadowing the diaspora but in a random fashion. In Cat Hill I first encountered a sort of middle class settled affluence and creativity that I felt at home in.

I made some drawings for my application, drawing objects on my windowsill. I had never had an art lesson in my life so I just did what I wanted, not trying to make it too arty. I was quite pleased with the results. Remembering half-hearted applications, I had made before, to Maidstone and Canterbury art schools, I imagined that again I would be exposed as a fraud by my interviewer.

I needn't have worried; the interviewer was interested in everything I had done. He didn't seem bothered that I wasn't coming from A level art and that my 'portfolio' was homespun. To his credit he decided to give me a chance. By autumn I had a grant and was starting out on my real education.

Middlesex Polytechnic had been formed by the amalgamation of the notorious Hornsey College of Arts and Crafts and two other local colleges. Hornsey had achieved notoriety because of all night protests and sit-ins during the summer of 1968, which were copied in art schools around the UK. Students occupied the Crouch End Hill site and during the six weeks that the riots lasted, Hornsey became the focus of debate about the method of art education and teaching in Britain. Students at the college convened to discuss the withdrawal of Student Union funds and resolved to sit-in. They took control of the college and called for a major review of the art curriculum. Supported by sympathetic academic staff and visiting artists they offered a critique of the education system, but the college was repossessed by local authorities at the beginning of the summer break. It was a very English rebellion and it ended with a whimper, but the memory of rebellion and occupation sustained through the punk years and beyond. When I went to Middlesex in 1986 several of the staff were old timers from Hornsey and their attitude to art deeply affected me. I had found a way home.

Before starting our Foundation year, we were sent some exercises to undertake which included a directive to choose a show and write about it. Almost at random I picked an Eduardo Paolozzi exhibition at the Museum of Mankind, a satellite department of the British Library which housed and exhibited their ethnographic collection. The museum was in a building on Burlington Gardens, behind the Royal Academy and I already knew and loved it. It was full of objects that seemed to hold out clues for my own work, to hint at the potential for making jewellery by a process of accretion. It was around the corner from Cork Street which, a street of commercial art galleries which I liked to visit, thinking they somehow represented the art world.

The show I saw was Lost Magic Kingdoms and Six Paper Moons. To create it Paolozzi had been given free run of the ethnographic collection. He had taken a range of items from the stores and placed them in museum vitrines with a variety of his own sculptures.

I understood the work immediately. I stood in front of it thinking, 'That's what I do. That's what I make'. I had been building assemblages of items, arranging them and photographing them, for years without ever really knowing what I was doing. I'd continued this behaviour while in Crete, collecting flotsam from the beach and building structures with it. I'd never thought of it as connected to my jewellery, although it suddenly seemed obvious that similar desires were at play.

In that dark space I finally got it. If this is art, then this is what I do. I make art. I knew then that I would make art rather than jewellery. Again, my life changed by epiphany. It took many years for me to realise this was how I worked, this was part of the disorder that drove my life, and my father's before me. A sudden realisation, a connecting of the dots followed by hyperactivity — then, later, loss of attention, lack of focus and abandonment, moving on. But for now, I had found art and art gave me a new way of finding what I wanted to do.

The art world of the 1980s was a poor second cousin to New York. In the seventies the 'scandal' of Carl Andre's Equivalent IV, better known as the 'Pile of Bricks' had held the nation in rapt attention, egged on by the tabloids, while failing to educate them in any fashion. That was the point, art was mad, bad and dangerous to know. The Prostitution show at the ICA in the Mall had heralded the punk era and provided a grateful tabloid press with a new generation of targets. The formula was always the same, from poking fun (literally) at the holes in Barbara Hepworth's work in the fifties to mocking Andre's bricks in the seventies, the papers ran riot. Since before Picasso, the popular press had known that artists could provide good copy, that mocking or taunting them and their supposed weirdnesses went down well with the public. When I first arrived in London I was vaguely aware of the wider art world but not the history or the reality of making art. I didn't think of myself as anything like an artist and I certainly didn't consider the things I made as art. Contemporary art was a rarefied pastime and few people were interested. Any attempts I made to create complex objects were driven by a desire to be allowed to make things.

I was an idiot savant.

I knew nothing of art when I went in but it all seemed quite obvious. Eduardo Paolozzi still echoed in my mind and I started collecting object and assembling them in my space. At the same time, I learnt to use the woodshop and the metal shop and a bunch of other tools. I started making slides by hand. I'm not sure where this idea came from, but I realised I could create huge sets of slides and put them into the round carousels that slide projectors used to use. When projected at speed in combination I could create something that seemed to come near to a projected film. I was entranced by the harshness of abstract images that looked somehow as if they were more than their abstraction.

I made my first piece of art that directly referenced the Holocaust, although I didn't really know what I was doing it. I welded a huge throne like chair form found rusting steel and hung a lightshade over it. After mounting various other found objects made of wood and glass on it I realised it looked like a torture implement and called it Josef Mengele, His Chair. I was inspired still by the torture device Franz Kafka a describes in The Penal Colony, a device into which the accused was strapped and which then engraved the nature of their crimes onto their body. Although I didn't want to build this machine, I was interested in the extremism of the thought.

At the end of my year, my mother suggested I might like to go and stay and work with an old friend of hers who lived in Southern Spain. I liked the idea, to get out of grey England for the summer and to hang out with an artist in the sunshine. I was buzzing with ideas and eager to continue to work over the summer, so I packed up and caught a train south to work in the sun for a few months. I was now travelling on a British passport and had completely forgotten my run in with the French authorities a year's previously.

This woman lived in a little house in a village as far south as it was possible to go after her husband had died. She gave me a tiny room at the back of the house, but I soon found out there wasn't really anything for me to do. I had become used to using workshop equipment, photographic kit and working with objects I found in skips and by poking around old buildings. None of that existed in this village. She made sculptures in clay and then cast them in plaster. I did learn how to use these tools, to make moulds from clay models, but after a few weeks I was climbing up the walls.

While I was marooned in the hot south of Spain my parents bought themselves a little house in the south of France. My mother, who remained a French national and a devoted French-woman, wanted a holiday house in France. As my father was retired and had recovered slowly but eventually well from his aneurysm, she insisted and eventually got her way. They bought a tiny slice of terraced house in a village in the foothills of the Pyrenees. The village, La Roc de Fa, was a Cathar village, part of the territory of a heresy against the Roman church which had swept the south of Europe in the middle ages. The Cathars were fiercely repressed by the Catholic church and had disappeared from history, although it was said that there were still secret adherents in the hills.

My parents went down to stay in their newly acquired house for the first time. I told my artist host that I was going to visit them. I booked a bus ticket and left. The bus took two days to get to the French border. The passengers consisted almost entirely of old women who were going into France, but I met a French guy and we sat together. When the bus got to the border a guard came on and walked down the coach. When he saw us sitting together and asked for our passports. I handed over my British passport. I had got used to being a Brit when travelling and I had forgotten about my scrape with French national service.

After a while the guard returned, looked at me and beckoned for me to follow him off the bus. I followed him into the small border office where the French policeman behind the desk gave me a quizzical look. 'Vous êtes français?' he said. Caught completely unawares I could only nod in agreement. They called a third border guard in, a large bulky guy wearing the insignia of the French paratroopers, the regiment of the nationalist Le Pen who was stirring up trouble. This guard was much less friendly and he bawled a stream of French at me, all the while shaking his head. He locked me into a small cell where I sat for a few hours, slowly realising that no matter what the authorities were going to do to me, I had a big problem on my hands. I had arranged to meet my parents in Perpignan where the bus would terminate in a couple of hours. Now the bus had gone off without me on it and I had no way of contacting them. They had no phones, I had no phone, mobile phones didn't exist. I was scared and lost and my anxiety kicked in as I sat in the tiny cell in the mid-day heat.

The local police turned up, an officer and a boy in a kepi. They put me in their tiny blue Renault and drove me away from the border and down a motorway at high speed while the boy tried to talk to me in broken English. We eventually arrived at a quiet police station. It was Saturday afternoon and we seemed to be the only people there. They gave me a chair and a coffee and set to work with their typewriters, teleprinters and phones.

After several hours of silent waiting, they raised an answer to their question: what do we do with this man? They showed me the answer that had come. It stated that I was a deserter from the French army and that I had a ten-month prison sentence awarded in absentia. This reply seemed to upset them; it clearly wasn't what they wanted. They had no idea what to do with me. They started a vigorous discussion amongst themselves about the situation while I sat and tried to understand what they were saying. Eventually they told me that I had to go to Paris to regularise my situation. They typed up a formal card. 'This man has been absent without leave for seven years, please deal with him accordingly'. Then they said I was free to go. The only problem was, I had no idea where I was or where I was going — and I had no French money. I made this clear to them in no uncertain fashion by throwing all my Spanish change onto the table and shouting at them.

The boy policeman told me he would drive me into town. Moments later the officer pulled rank on him, so we all piled back into the little Renault and they drove me into town and dropped me off at the main square.

I turned up at Goldsmiths with no idea of what was going to happen. I had no knowledge of who was already there or what sort of work the place was known for and precious little knowledge of or interest in the wider art world, except. I was ready to work, eager to explore my recent discoveries more, but beyond that I waited to see what the place would throw at me.

The art school was situated in a place called Myatt's Fields, in the quiet no-man's land between Camberwell and Brixton. Exiled since 1973 to a red brick building, far from the watching eyes of the Warden, we were free to get on with what we wanted. We drifted in the backwash of half understood post-modernist theoreticians such as Derrida and Lacan. The college was well known for its generous admissions policy that didn't make students nominate a discipline to follow. 'I went there,' Damien Hirst later said, 'because they didn't ask whether you were a painter or a sculptor.' I went for exactly the same reason.

Our college building was a rabbit warren of corridors and rooms in an elegant redbrick building that had been a teacher training establishment. It was tucked away in the backstreets of Brixton next to a small park called Mya 's Fields, it was far away from the main university site in New Cross. We might as well have been an independent college. Sometimes it felt like we were orbiting a spaceship far out in space.

In addition to fine art the building contained the textiles department that had so inspired me and the workshops for both schools. In the basement was a bar and small restaurant where temping chefs cooked the most appalling food. The basement also contained the woodwork and metal workshops. The metal workshop had a fully functioning foundry for casting metal alongside the usual panoply of welding and cutting gear. The textiles department had their own studios and workshops. I soon discovered that I was free to use either, nobody questioned what I was doing.

I was keen to build more large-scale sculptures and to experiment with found materials, following on from the success of my constructed pieces at Middlesex. Beyond that I had little idea of where my work was going. I did know that I had something, that I could produce reactions with my work. I was determined to continue to do that. I was also interested in making more installations, using light and dark, slides and film, as I had briefly experimented with at Middlesex.

I was allocated a share of a room on an upper floor with a bunch of painters and the like. In anticipation of making work from found objects I had acquired a van during the summer and I soon put it to work, cruising the West End at night and pulling wood, glass and metal out of skips. As my small space started to overflow with tut my tutor, Ferris Newton, took me aside. He asked me what sort of things I was making and after I told him he rustled me up a much larger space in the basement alongside a guy who carved tree trunks with a chainsaw and a painter who spent the whole year sitting in an armchair looking at his work.

At first I lived with some art students near the college. My old friend, Lyndsey, asked if I wanted to move in to her flat in Peckham. Lindsey had moved from Tunbridge Wells years before and, in a sort of echo of my short life days, had ended up in a squat with her boyfriend. The flat was the top floor of a ruined yet elegant building on Choumert Road. Peckham was considered beyond the pale but I was happy to move there. There was nothing I wanted more and I upped and left the over excited art school atmosphere for the rarefied top floor of a Peckham slum. The squat had been given legitimacy by the landlord but the rent was miniscule and I paid a paltry sum for everything. That said, although the place was dry and reasonably clean, it had no bathroom. There was a bath in the kitchen with a wooden lid that folded up and the kitchen sink was used for washing up and toile e. The flat had a hatch which gave access to the roof and we spent a lot of time sunning ourselves while overlooking the street. To me it seemed like a chunk of heaven.

At the end of that first year, it was announced that the course was moving to the main site for the following year. The college had built a new library at New Cross which had cleared space to move Fine Art and Textiles into the vacated space of the old library. This had been the plan all along and it released the building for sale, but the building we started in had come to seem like a hermetically sealed spaceship, taking our art experiments further and further away from the main site and because we knew that whatever they came up with for the new site would never be as good. They declared they would move all the workshops and studios over the summer holidays and build new facilities on the back fields of the main site. They also decided to build a new studio block, but we knew they wouldn't. At the end of the year, we cleared our studios and put anything we wanted transferred into a storage room at the back of the building. We said goodbye to our spaceship.

3

Young British Anarchists

When we reconvened at college for the new year, in September 1988, it was at the main site in New Cross. The studios were in chaos and the workshops unbuilt. The atmosphere of being in a calm art bubble of the previous year was completely gone. Now we were now just one group of students on a much bigger campus, sharing facilities with others.

Something else changed. The students in the year above us had organised a show of their own in an abandoned building out in the docklands and were getting serious media attention. The college took us out to docklands to see it.

It was Damien Hirst's now famous show, Freeze. By the time we returned from that uneventful trip, although we didn't yet know it, we had been irrevocably divided into two groups: those who believed in a superstar future and those who would fight tooth and nail for something more realistic. Without realising it I had fallen into the second group.

In his studio, Hirst had already produced an embryonic spot painting and was working on a sculpture '... filled with drugs from my grandmother's medicine cabinet that she gave me before she died,' he explained. He called it Sinner. Years later his mother Mary, telling how she fell pregnant as a Catholic unmarried mother, cheerfully explained, 'Damien was my sin.'

The school had no rigid philosophy and no careerist approach that would lead to success in the art world. In my first year my tutor, Ferris Newton, an elegant American artist, told me that the college was waiting for another Julian Opie, an artist who had gone from Goldsmiths to almost immediate art world success, something that was considered incredibly rare but necessary for the college's esteem. On the whole it was expected that students would plough through the course making a series of unholy messes and graduate elegantly before thinking seriously about what to do next. Arcane art practices such as performance, installation and video thrived in a crazy messy collaborative environment. Well known for its serious metal and wood shops and casting foundry, Goldsmiths also contained its own bar, deep in the basement of the hulk. Open from mid-afternoon until the early hours of the morning, it provided sustenance for the body and soul and was run with an iron rod by an ex-student, Angie. Hirst was an enthusiastic if irregular visitor.

'He worked a lot but used to arrive and demand a drink immediately. If I pointed out that there was a queue, he would just take a glass and pull his own pint,' she said. He ran up a bar tab even though such a thing was unknown. When she asked him to pay it off, he offered her one of the collages that were on show in the bar.

'I pointed to one that I liked. He said it was twenty pounds, exactly what he owed. I took it.'

Hirst was also a different kind of student. Manipulating those around him with an easy charm, he was always up to something, involved in things with his clubby group, mostly northerners. He'd come down from Leeds a couple of years earlier after being turned down by St Martins, and had hung around, working on building sites and in a telephone marketing operation. A hard worker who earned his own money, it taught him the skills needed to persuade strangers to buy what you had. That skill was to come in very useful sooner than anyone imagined.

A part time job at Anthony D'Offay's gallery, one of the pre-eminent dealers of eighties London art, gave him an insider's eye for the art world. He was already trying out various strategies. "What I learned from the job was that I wanted to be able to afford a roll of bubble wrap to wrap my own work."

As the college drifted through 1988, Hirst developed his own trajectory. Gathering a growing group of students around him, he worked first with fellow student Angus Fairhurst on a small show at the Institute of Education. Inspired by shows at the huge Saatchi gallery on Boundary Road, he sought the use of a building in east London from the Docklands Development Corporation. Flushed with redevelopment fervour, they had offered him a vacated Port of London Authority building two miles due north from Goldsmiths.

Freeze took place between the beginning of August and early September 1988. The students had scraped and painted and cleaned the building. Seventeen of them, they included many of who would later become the Young British Artists, the YBAs.

That year they were enthusiastic amateurs who knew how to throw a party.

Damien had raised money for the catalogue from various sponsors, including developers Olympia and York.

'What could you possibly think of to do in an enormous white space with four old ladies, a solid oak table, a meat axe and a stopwatch?' Hirst asked in a letter to potential participants. After producing the catalogue, he used what was left over to transport luminaries from the art world to the show. The myth of Charles Saatchi on the back of a taxi motorbike gained currency among art students in the years that followed. His show got a single review, in the Guardian, from a young critic, Sacha Craddock.

'I took the bus out to the show with Jon Thompson, head of art, and Damien himself. Jon kept telling me how good Hirst was. The space was incredible, unlike any student show I'd ever seen, and they pressed a proper catalogue into my hands. The next day Damien was round at my house, giving me photos of the work. He was a star.'

Along with most observers, Craddock saw Hirst as the curator and she gave him a scarily prescient accolade: Organised by Damien Hirst ... it succeeds perhaps because ruthless decisions have been made by one person, but maybe the very nature of art school products has changed in order to reflect the set-piece one-liner that succeeds in the commercial world.

Before Hirst, Goldsmiths was stuck in an eighties rut. The US had led the art world since the fifties, since before the fifties. The sixties wave of artists who came out of swinging London were well established but dull. A generation of artists who had come to prominence at the end of the seventies and the beginning of the eighties were not creating waves. London was still an art centre, but it was dominated by an older group of dealers, each with their own stable of artists. In the way of the world, as with music and politics, this hermetic world watched and waited for the next development.

From the outside art colleges looked like generators of strangeness—from the inside they were like a cult headquarters. Everything that I had ever been interested in suddenly came together in an environment where I was judged only on doing interesting things. I couldn't own this space, it was already tied up and controlled by others, but if I wanted to, if I put my mind to it I could carve out a piece of it for myself. And there were many options, many ways forward. Art didn't offer a stable career, but then I'd never looked for that. I didn't even really know that such a thing existed. I was still high on rebellion, on punk attitude, and I carried the do it yourself approach of the end of the seventies into my art world life and beyond.

Colleges themselves had similarly lost much of their revolutionary fervour. The London colleges that attracted the most attention were Chelsea, where large painting was the order of the day, and St Martins, still basking in the reflected glory of the punk years. The central location of St Martins and Central made them attractive bases for ambitious students. Goldsmiths, stuck out on the fringes, didn't have the cachet, and wasn't considered a key art school. All the same, a college system that had produced many pop superstars and generations of successful artists didn't think it had much to prove. Students still got grants rather than loans, and other support measures were reasonably generous.

A key but remote player in this pantomime was Michael Craig-Martin, an American artist and teacher who had come to Goldsmiths in 1973 when, as he said, 'the school had a terrible reputation for being anarchic'.

He was a popular figure in the college among those who were his students but to most of us he was a remote figure who showed no interest in our work. He had picked up his group and they now had privileges — not that any of that occurred to me at the time. I was in full punk rock mode, mocking, scorning, running around enjoying myself. I failed to see the opportunity to make serious work and escalate from art college. Craig-Martin and the other tutors, on the other hand, fully understood the opportunity that Hirst had opened up and they were determined to run through the opening. In 2011 Craig-Martin explained what happened for the Goldsmiths alumni magazine.

'Then, in 1978, suddenly the department was decamped into this amazing place, Mya Field, which had been a teacher training college. Suddenly everything was brought together and it became a hothouse dynamo. In the early 80s there were some young people, like Julian Opie and Lisa Milroy, who, for the first time, were having success in the outside world. It became possible for the kids at Goldsmiths to see that you could go to Goldsmiths and have a life, a visible life, as an artist. And then the pinnacle of that came in the mid to late 80s which is really when the YBA [Young British Artists] thing happened.

'It's like everything else in life that seems like it happened overnight — it took 10 years before you knew about it. Nobody really expected the amazing thing that happened.

'I tried to mix the students which generated a kind of dialogue amongst them. They were getting used to looking at each other's work in depth and also of being jealous of each other and being competitive in the best possible way. If I did a seminar and Sarah Lucas did something fantastic, then Gary Hume was pissed off because she got all the attention and he wanted it — it's a normal human thing, but it had an amazing effect. One of the things that was incredibly good fortune for all of them was Damien doing Freeze. They were all doing diverse things but Freeze gave them a group identity. Then subsequently, everything that happened to one of them, helped all the others.

After Goldsmiths had reeled the art department back into the mother ship at New Cross and the Freeze show had thrown down a gauntlet of commercialism, the college started to crackle with energy, though it seemed for a long while unsure of where to direct this energy or from whence it originated. There were battles to come.

At art college, to my surprise, nobody told you how to find a way to make art or to find a subject. They didn't even tell you how to go about the process of making art, of starting work. It was left to some unknowable internal process and we all got on with it as if we also understood. I didn't know what I was supposed to be making art about. I had some ideas but they all seemed dangerous. Making work was a tricky game where you had to end up in a unique space between the obvious and the completely obscure. Later I worked out for myself that art was a meme field and art school was intended to introduce us to the elements of that field.

A meme is a unit of information that is passed from person to person. It contains a value to each person to acquires it and an inherent reason to pass it on. I felt that this explained the art world and gave me some clarity on what we were doing, although the realisation came many years too late to be of use. In fact, I had no idea of how to speak with art. I had quickly understood the visual memes and worked out which I liked and which I didn't. The trick was to copy the memetic tropes that you liked, combining them as you liked, but to introduce a new element such that your work was both identifiable as art while at the same time seeming to be entirely new. Thus, the people who mattered would understand your provenance and could place your work within a continuity. This was harder than it sounds.

I understood that writing with words and making work with objects were more or less the same things, or they allowed you to speak, if you wish, about the same things. My problem still was that while I had plenty of things to speak about when I looked for a subject, a something to express as an artist, I was scared or, rather, my subject was rebellion, of which I was not scared and about which I could express myself eloquently. But that wasn't seen as art, not yet. I was still making that journey with a destination but no map that I'd made back from Athens, trying not to let the existential terrors of the night get to me, trying to keep warm and fed and keep moving because the destination is always there. I've kept doing this my whole life, I've never finished an artwork, I've never finished a book, I keep pushing my life ahead of me like a glacier carving out rocks and shunting them forward so that they eventually will form a long barrier of hills, like the Downs that I live on the edge of, which will sustain centuries after I have melted like the glacier. Then people will wonder, how did this line of memory come to be place here and slowly, like geologists, they will work it out. He was a glacier.

On the main campus in the new studios were in chaos and the workshops absent. There was a new world order: on the back of the Freeze show, a small group had started the climb to stardom from our midst. The rest of the college was in various states of disaffection. In the face of the activities of a small group of students and the escalating media attention, the college seemed to lose its collective mind. We had returned to the predicted chaos. No workshops were ready and the studios were half built. The new studio block on the back field was incomplete and weeks passed with little work. We hung around, frustrated while the antics of the putative Hirst gang garnered more media attention. The students involved had largely disappeared, but we still had to make our way through our degrees in a half-built landscape.

I went to the student union and asked them for help, and they suggested we call a one-day strike. I realised that I knew the perfect timing for this. Although Goldsmiths listed itself as a college of the University of London, it had never been a full college and existed still as something of a satellite loner in South London. Repeated attempts to join with the powerful London University had failed but had taken a toll over the years. Sciences at

Goldsmiths had been described as a 'pimple on the face of South London' which led to the rapid defenestration of chemistry and other courses. This sudden clearing out of established services had led to the strange environment that the computer labs occupied: the redundant labs had been pressed to use for this new world. I knew nothing of computers at the time, I was just interested in causing some trouble. I heard that Goldsmiths had finally been granted its wish of full membership of LU and an historic event had been organised: a visit by the Chancellor of the University, none other than Princess Anne, to seal the deal. A general meeting of the student body was called and when we gathered in the great hall I proposed a one-day strike on the day the Princess was due to visit. The call was carried overwhelmingly and it drove a stake deep into the institutional heart of the college. I hadn't forgotten the lessons that punk taught me.

In order to progress our cause, the Union alerted the South London Press, a despicable local rag, who sent a couple of reporters along to hear our story. They showed no interest in our story, but as they were leaving I briefly told them about something else I knew about. It seemed that as part of Anne's visit she needed to be shown around the college art gallery. A problem had transpired: the show then on contained a large painting called Porsche Cabriolet, its image was of a Porsche car and a man with a large erection. This was deemed unacceptable for the royal visit and I had heard that the entire show would be taken down and replaced with a harmless college Pissarro and other impressionists. The reporters perked up a bit and set out for the gallery. I met them shortly afterwards, giggling and carrying a copy of the exhibition catalogue.

A couple of days after this visit, the college caved in completely to our demands and agreed to pay an allowance to every art student in order that they could continue their studies without working, during the holidays. This demand was my invention. The idea that many of us would have jobs over the Easter holidays was preposterous, but we lined up at the Bursar's office and every one of us was handed two weeks' worth of grant money -- in cash. The strike was called off, but our activity still had unforeseen consequences.

The gallery show had been taken down and replaced in time for the visit the following week, but to my horror (mixed with pleasure), on the morning of the visit the Sun newspaper led with a huge headline, GET HIM ORF, and a reproduction of the Porsche Cabriolet picture with a CENSORED banner over the man's cock. The story started with the line, 'Fine Art bigwig, Peter Cresswell, was in trouble today as the royal visit caused the removal of a rude picture'. The story was picked up by many other newspapers including the Guardian, causing embarrassment all round. Creswell was the head of my part of the college. I decided to keep my head down and I never admitted any role in the story.

I complained a lot about the lack of tutors, about how they were ignoring us. In reality I had difficulty relating to these people in the same way that I always found it difficult to know how to talk to my peers who were supposedly my superiors. That might be why I never could get a job. My first-year tutor was an American artist called Ferris Newton, who seems to have disappeared without trace. We got on well and he liked my approach to work, helping me out where he could. My subsequent tutor,

Mark Wallinger, was only two years older than me but far advanced in the art world. That they even understood there was an art world is probably a clue to my inability to connect. Although I was now immersed in the cult of art I still hadn't really twigged that you needed to be proactive. If the attitude I later took to my businesses could have been replicated at that moment with my art I might have flown out of Goldsmiths on golden wings, like Hirst himself. I could have made myself into a brand. But none of that occurred to me. I was stuck back in my internal world and my fear of communication. My tutorials with Mark, infrequent as they were, consisted of us sitting side by side in almost silence while we both struggled to find something to say about my work. A few years later he would lose out to Damien Hirst for the Turner prize, but nevertheless go on to create a good art career for himself outside the YBA hothouse.

I was trying to find a way to let some things inside me out while fitting into my concept of what it was to be an artist. This was harder said than done in an atmosphere where half the college seemed to hate the art world and the other half were desperately trying to work out how to become part of it. One day I wrote down on a piece of paper, 'I am a collector of Nazi memorabilia'. I was trying to rationalise my interest in the Holocaust and to progress from the work I had made in my foundation year, *Josef Mengele, His Chair*.

I liked the ring of the new phrase I had written, I liked that it seemed transgressive, that it implied that I had an interest in Nazi material (which I did) while allowing the reader to work out that it was not because I was a Nazi. Even more, I liked the idea of being a collector of memorabilia. Of course, I never literally collected anything like that, I had no medals or belts or badges and had no interest in them, but my mind would insist on collecting references and ideas about this time. Eventually I built a book collection on the subject which seemed safe and useful. The work I Am a Collector of Nazi Memorabilia is still ongoing, I've been making it for thirty years now without ever finding a form or even doing much work on it. It resides within me, floating, waiting, allowing a lot of other things to happen. And then, I believe that I have only ever made one piece of work and am still remaking it and will continue to do so throughout my life. I didn't know this when it seemed to matter and I'm not sure what use it is now. Maybe it only allows me to still be an artist, to not join those sad ranks of those who have made themselves give up art, as if their youthful attendance at art school was some sort of foible, some sort of silly aberration and that no rational person makes art.

After the unexpected success of my rebellion, I looked around for another opportunity to make a stink. Just over a month after the Freeze show, a third-year student, Rachel Stelmach, started a newsletter called, Spotlight, ostensibly to document and promote work from the experimental side of college. The rag charted events and contention over one college year, 26 issues. The publication charts both viscerally and visually the precise changes that took place over that time as it mutates from a single side written and hand typed by the founder to a computer generated free for all in which sides are taken and colours nailed to masts. The key change, portending a switch from the past to the future, comes between issues eleven and twelve. In number eleven the editor encloses a supplement that I wrote about Freeze, headed So What's Going On III and hints at a 'smarter, glossier, sleeker bulletin'. The next issue, twelve, is produced with computer software that the designers are clearly barely able to use. It is a design disaster, but a beautiful experiment. The chasm had been leapt; the future had been seized. A column headed Don't Fear The Computer talked of the Computer Department's 'well-kept secret' and Rachel's editorial stated, 'Praise be to technology. I now have a co-editor (Ivan) without whom the conversion to this technology might not have taken place'.

I still had my punk attitude, which kept me in trouble. It was a cover for any insecurity I felt, for my inability to network and to understand what I needed to do to get ahead. It was also, as I found out much later, a symptom of the disorder, at that point totally undiagnosed, the disorder had a good side doing its work alongside the bad side. I was in a creative frenzy, but this creativity manifested itself in political rebellion as much as the making of artworks.

I believed in writing and publishing and being noisy and the newsletter reminded me of fanzines so I offered to contribute. The newsletter started in October 1988 at the beginning of the new school year. It was put together using traditional punky cut and paste, typed and drawn directly onto the page and copied up in the college print shop. It was related to a weekly event that had been running for the previous year, before the caesura of the move, putting on a wide range of activities: 'Animated films, books, installations, live music, musical premiers, performances, group and individual poetry readings, power breakfasts, recording sessions, revivalist evenings, sixteen mm films, slide dissolve, sound, Super 8, tapes, video showings.' The event almost defines the last days of what art colleges had become, a mixture of the radical and invented media of the sixties and seventies. It was a world that was about to be largely swept away, or at least made irrelevant by events taking place in the same college.

The first column I wrote, in November 1988, riffed off the geography of the new site and our disaffection at being so far from the main site and the action. To be honest, the new studio, once it was finished, was a good place to work and I stayed in it for the next two years, having my degree show there, but it was isolated. There was a growing feeling that we were missing something, that things were happening that the college didn't want us involved with. A sense of disaffection and anticipation started to grow. The Spotlight newsletter was very much an outsider publication, it covered what had become traditional and most of those making this sort of work eschewed the Damien Hirst clique. They had, anyway, to all intents and purposes, disappeared.

At the end of the month, I addressed the perceived absence of tutors in a column titled Spot the Tutor. 'It has come to my attention that many of you have been playing that new popular game, 'Spot the Tutor'. Prizes range from the simple Tutorial right up to the top of the range Exhibition of work with Seminar. The following week, after talking to technicians about the failure to install basic equipment in the workshops, I wrote a satirical piece about the installation of gas piping in the metal shop. Possibly sensing some hostility building and aware of the dangerous enemies I may make, I added a disclaimer, 'The events and personalities in this story are set firmly in never-never land. They have absolutely no basis in the real world and bear no relationship to any characters either living or dead or working at Goldsmiths College.'

The first inkling of my new incarnation as computer guru came in January 1989 with the first issue of Spotlight of that year.

'You will all be receiving an extra page to this week's bulletin. This is partly because there was a far greater materialisation of writing than I had expected so early in the term and also as a test run on some of the desk-top publishing facilities which I have been looking at along with Ivan and there may soon be a new smarter, glossier, sleeker bulletin on its way to you. On the other hand, it might not be so easy. One can but try, is that not so?'

It was not easy, but we had stumbled across something new. The old world of cut and paste was being overthrown and a digital space invented, all in tandem with a ramping up of the rhetoric of contention. Rachel and I soon became fixtures in the computer lab. We taught ourselves how to use the publishing tools and scanners and printers, there really was nobody else to teach us, it was autodidact or die. We learnt fast though, and within a few issues we were incorporating images and fancy fonts. It had been a tough rite of passage but suddenly everything opened up in front of us.

My provocations continued and escalated, possibly because there was little response from the institution who were by now enraptured of the Hirst clique in our midst. In February I mocked an interview that Michael Craig-Martin had done for the Late Show in our studios. My provocations were working and the Newsletter became a battleground for the variety of views in the art department. Words like deconstruction, Thatcherism, polarisation were bandied about. Rachel wrote a pieced headed There Is No Such Thing As Society, Only A Collection Of Individuals. And then someone invented Anti-freeze.

I still feel my heart jump into my mouth at my presumptuousness. I knew that I was pushing at what the department held most dear, but I felt there were no outlets for protest and that the place had become stagnant. More than that, it had awarded a huge number of firsts the previous year and everyone knew this connected precisely to commercial success. This was not what art school was supposed to be about, although in many ways I was merely missing the new point of art college. But I found I was not alone and the revolution that I hoped to engender was starting to create waves with angry responses and now, from another student, Marea Coss, a polemic on the response of the college to the tension over the move and Damien Hirst's Docklands' Freeze show. She called the article 'Anti-Freeze' and in doing so created a phrase that was later often mistakenly attributed to me and held against me as evidence of my hostility to the whole new Goldsmiths project.

The world was changing, and me with it.

Great changes usually come out of nowhere and the moments of their inception are seldom remembered, but I know exactly when my life switched from analogue to digital, though it would be a slow switchover. I discovered a tool that would change the world. It threw me back into publishing, back into talking to the world. Not that I understood this at first, I just liked the idea of Desktop Publishing more than was decent. Something in them sparked life into me. They connected me across time and space to the hot metal machines in the basement of the Standard and to the newspapers that always came home with daddy. I wasn't alone either, there were others who got it and we instinctively formed a group of acolytes. This led to my immersion in computing and to the online world and to everything that followed. We discovered Desktop Publishing and this led to my immersion in computing and to the online world and to everything that followed.

One day as I crossed the area of grass known as the Back Field, someone told me that in the computer centre there was 'a machine that can do columns'. I wasn't entirely ignorant of trends in publishing. I had a small obsession with DTP and had been reading about it, so the tip off was well aimed.

I found my way up to the computer centre which turned out to be an abandoned science lab, with all the science infrastructure still in situ. It didn't seem strange as I was more used to science labs than to computer labs, of which I knew nothing. The two rooms had a few computers and printers do ed about. I located an employee called Roy and asked about this computer that *could do columns.*

He took me over to a grey machine with an A4 screen and a laser printer a ached and told me that the person who had bought the system had left soon afterwards and 'nobody knows how to use it'. The machine ran a program called Ventura. He turned it on and attempted to show me how it worked, but it soon became clear he didn't really know how it worked. I summoned Rachel and between us we started a long process of autodidactic back and forth.

Although we had no idea how to use this thing, the fact that it had a laser printer that could output graphics and that it was designed to make layouts made us determined to use it for the newsletter. We set about producing the next issue while struggling with a conceptual void. Nobody knew how to make anything happen and although we quickly found out how to type text in and lay it out on the page, doing anything more complex seemed impossible that first week.

We managed to produce a newsletter using our new technology and although I didn't know where it was headed, everything had changed. I had found computers; I had found a computer centre and I had stumbled across people who worked with this stuff every day.

Without looking for it the next low door in the wall was finally opening.

4

Epiphany

1990

ARPANET ceases to exist

Electronic Frontier Foundation (EFF)is founded by Mitch Kapor Archie released by Peter Deutsch, Alan Emtage, and Bill Heelan at McGill

Hytelnet released by Peter Scott (Univ of Saskatchewan) The World comes on-line (world.std.com), becoming the first commercial provider of Internet dial-up access

Czechoslovakia (.cs) connects to EARN/BitNet (11 Oct); .cs deleted in 1993

Countries connecting to NSFNET: Argentina (AR), Austria (AT), Belgium (BE), Brazil (BR), Chile (CL), Greece (GR), India (IN), Ireland (IE), Korea (KR), Spain (ES), Switzerland (CH) [Hobbes' Internet Timeline]

Then I made a breakthrough.

I wasn't looking for it but I discovered a new world. It was a real Eureka moment. I didn't think of it like that at the time, of course, but it changed everything.

Because I was spending so much time in the computer labs I started helping out other students and became adept at the word processing program of the time, Wordperfect, and even learnt something of the DOS operating system. The department started asking me to cover evening support sessions and then weekends. I was soon picking up the keys for the computer lab on Saturdays and opening the whole thing up. I spent a lot of time during these sessions nosing around in all the rooms. After all, I had the keys for everything and I wanted to find out what there was in the place.

I became fascinated by a little Apple Mac that I found in the back room and soon I discovered that there was a magazine called Wheels for the Mind, an Apple sponsored publication for the academic world. In this I came across an article about email-based Apple support groups: Info-Mac and Mac-Supporters. I read the article in detail and it sounded fascinating. The only problem was, I had no idea what it was talking about. It said that in order to access these email groups I would need access to a system called JANET.

It said I would need *email*. I would have to send commands to this address. I would get to join a list of people and I could ask them questions. I didn't understand what I was reading, but it lit a small light bulb over my head. I went to the guys who ran the computers and showed them the article.

'Janet,' they said, knowingly. 'Sure, we can make you an account.'

They gave me the ID 'art1'. I was the first person from the art faculty who had ever asked for an account. They told me I could use a bunch of terminals in the old science lab to email my lists.

I had absolutely no idea what I had been given access to or how to use it. I took the magazine and sat down at the nearest computer.

The computers that had a connection to the networks were used by the psychology and geography departments to crunch research data. They were dumb terminals, computer screens with no intelligence that were connected by a network to the bigger computers that did the work. None of the other computers in the department were networked at all at this point, they all stood isolated in their lab. Indeed, the whole idea of personal or desktop computers was so new that the lab still had in daily use the very first IBM PC which had been launched a few years previously.

These terminals were a ached to a network and, through the college computers, a ached to the Janet network. They had green monotone screens. They used a command line interface, which meant all instructions had to be typed out in a specific language and format. I understood the idea because I'd learnt the PC version of this, which was called DOS, but it was still painfully like trying to write in a foreign language without even a phrase book. I'd never been any good at languages.

The screen emitted that eerie green glow of the type beloved by science fiction television programme makers. The commands

I had to type all started with CBS%. After that you typed the command.

It turned out that to send an email on the VAX/VMS machine you had to invoke the email program then write your text, then add the recipient's address and then fire your email towards a 'gateway' that would forward the missive on to another network, and thus to the recipient.

If there was ever a conceptual void, I was now in one. I had no idea what I was doing and no help beyond the magazine and a few leaflets about JANET to guide me. I sat in front of the machine, like a chimpanzee trying to teach itself myself a new language. I tried again and again and again, writing emails and seeing them bounce back as I failed to make them go anywhere. However dull this was, however frustrating, something at the back of my mind told me to keep trying. So, I did. I kept returning to the monitor and after a week or more, I somehow got my first ever email through the correct portal. I got a response.

My first ever email said, 'Help'. I got one reply.

'Come now Ivan, that's not very useful. What sort of help do you want?'

I stared at the screen. Somebody had replied. It worked.

The magic kicked in.

I typed 'Help, help, help, help, help.' I hit Return and waited. The next time I looked there were several replies. People from around the world were talking to me, replying to my email, giving me ideas and advice. They were friendly. I had made it through.

I stared into the screen, through the screen. A wave of realisation swept over me but it was the artist in me that understood what I had found. There was a world in there. This was an actual space, a place. I COULD MAKE WORK IN THERE I thought, in a blinding flash. In that moment of revelation, I saw and understood the world of cyberspace, the online planet. Eureka. I had it, I understood. If I had been naked in a bath I would have leapt out and run naked down the hall.

Later, my mind grappled with the potential of this new place. I had no real idea of how to access it, what to do with it or where it would lead, but I knew it was something real and that I had to explore it.

I was still an art student but the art world had nothing to do with computers, certainly at Goldsmiths. I started reading all I could about technology and art and looking for artists who were using this stuff.

In the college I quickly became a suspect, someone who had gone over to the dark side. Most people didn't know what I was on about, though a few showed some interest. I continued to make installations and to use the workshops and slowly ideas started to form in my mind for ways to take this forward.

Outside my computer centre bubble, where I was starting to become a fixture and to help people out with their essays, the Damien Hirst driven circus continued. What I was up to, nobody had a clue, it didn't make any sense to most people outside my tiny group. It was hard to find anyone who had an interest in using the technology outside their own coursework.

What I did hear several times that year was, 'Ivan's gone crazy, it's all computers with him now.'

Those first stumbles into the networks found a lot of tools like email, FTP, Usenet. There were artists online and they were making art. Of course, it figured, artists were always at the forefront of everything, they blazed the trail because they had nothing to gain and nothing to lose. Afterwards the commercial operators would sit up and notice and the artists would move on - or be forced to move on. The artists out there in the darkness and gave me my first reasons for playing online. I understood the idea of mail art, which was still popular at the time, and online artists were playing similar games. They sent images from person to person and modified them each time. I had found a community that I could associate myself with and a process that I understood. My online life was underway, but it was a struggle. There was no graphical interface like we're used to now, everything had to be done through a variety of methods and the dreaded command line interface started off most sessions. The college was connected to Janet by a tiny connection and it was still very difficult to pass things on.

I found various embryonic nodes of information, lists of things, and pushed out from there. After a while I realised that there were many networks of different types, from the academic internets to standalone bulletin boards, private communication hubs and homemade networks. I had stumbled on an entire world of communication.

In the publication that graduating students always make, this time titled Goldsmiths 1989, there are forty-five students. Several of them are still my friends. Some of them are dead. A few of them are world famous, many still work as successful artists even if you haven't heard of them.

The head of Fine Art, Jon Thompson, wrote his introduction that year, admitting that things had been difficult.

Booted out of our cosy red-brick Victorian mansion in Myatts Field — thick with birdsong and the smell of spring blossoms — after a restless summer we came to rest here in New Cross in accommodation which, at the time, bore more resemblance to a building site than to a School of Art.

For a time tempers burned on a short fuse. There was more talk of the wilful destruction of a famous school than there was of Fine Art practice and the complex issues which surround it. Like displaced persons everywhere, we were looking backwards rather than forwards, looking to the pleasures and achievements of the past as a way of easing the discomforts of the present. Certainly, for a spell, we were blind, or so it seemed, to all that the new site had to offer.

In retrospect this was an interesting time but fraught with danger. The Fine Art course could easily have torn itself apart, the internal stresses were so great. Now things look very different. Gradually, over December, January and February, the inherent strength of Fine Art here at Goldsmiths reasserted itself. Staff and students alike began to see the very real opportunities the move had opened up for broadening the base of the course and allowing it to reach into areas of activity which, because of the lack of facilities, were barely possible at the Camberwell site.

This, then, is the most rewarding feature of this year's degree exhibitions. Photography, film, video and performance work have emerged as equally important and compelling areas of activity, alongside our traditional strengths in painting and object-making.

In my view, this is the strongest show, overall, that students at Goldsmiths have produced and quite properly it sets a demanding standard for the future.

Thompson was right. Moving to the main campus had opened up areas of activity which were barely possible at the previous site. If we hadn't moved that year I wouldn't have been driven to such rebellion, I wouldn't have started writing about it, I wouldn't have discovered the computers, desk top publishing or, eventually, the internet. Serendipity is a powerful master and I had found my way forward.

Hirst and his cohort graduated at the end of my second year. While I was sinking further into the computer world, the Hirst generation prepared to step out onto the world stage. All the rules had changed. Student degree shows were always a moment of high drama for those involved, led up to by weeks of fevered speculation and production drama. Although there was literally a degree at stake, the opportunity to show one's work, to put up a semi-professional exhibition in white painted studios was more important. Depending on the stature of the college, and the vagaries of the art world, there was always the possibility that real gallery owners, actual dealers or collectors with cash would attend and notice your work and bestow their favour on you. If not, your uncle might buy a painting and give you a short breathing space before you had to go out and get a real job.

There was an air of frantic speculation in the air and, for some of them, the fantasy 'art world' that always existed just beyond the horizon, was now in the offing. The likelihood of a visit by collectors was not just fantasy stoked by desire, it was real. The name most bandied about was Charles Saatchi, one half of the Saatchi and Saatchi advertising duo, and a huge collector of contemporary art. Saatchi ran his own gallery on Boundary Road, a nod to American galleries and the inspiration for Hirst's commercial aspirations. Nobody in my circle would even have known what he looked like, how he dressed or how to recognise him if indeed he did materialise among us, but we fantasised about a visit, how Deus ex Machina, he would descend and buy our entire show and we would be made men. It was, of course, just a fantasy, but that year we came close enough to it to feel the heat and to smell the whiff of sulphur, because the devil incarnate did indeed descend into our midst and pluck the lucky few into a different world.

And then the golden generation were gone, off our backs, and we were free to luxuriate in our final year, to dream our dreams, to make our art, copycat or no, and work towards our own degree show.

I was living opposite the New Cross campus with my girlfriend, above a dry cleaners'. This made it easy to get to my studio but also easy to stay there all hours and ignore home life. I was immersed in fine art, in student life and in computers. Everything I had discovered fitted a need that I had, that I'd always had. I wanted to make things and I wanted to write things. I wanted to talk about the world and these were my ways of doing just that.

My studio was in a new building at the back of the fields behind the college. It was a big airy building where we hung out, piled up junk, made paintings, sculptures, installations. We sat outside the back door and drank beer, smoked dope, talked endlessly about art and how it fitted in the world. In the holidays I would go on working in the studio, mostly on my own, in total silence. The workshops were near my studio on the back field, metal and wood shops. Being on the main campus did open up access to new stuff, and the best of it was the computer centre.

As the end of the course approached I was spending a lot of my time in the computer centre. A lot. I had become the de facto teacher of desk top publishing and they started to give me shifts on user support. After a summer working on documentation, I became the weekend support person who opened up in the morning and closed it again afterwards. I enjoyed picking up the huge bunch of keys from the porters and being totally in control. The place was never very busy so I had plenty of time to nose around and find out what was in cupboards and offices. I found all sorts of obsolete networking kit and would trawl through cupboards and storerooms looking for useful bits.

One afternoon during a very quiet period I started wondering what was behind the big, locked doors in the other half of the building. I knew it was a psychology building. I sorted through my huge bunch of keys until I found one that opened the doors, but as they swung away from me, before I had a chance to step into the corridor behind, a mass of alarm bells started ringing. I had unwittingly opened up the animal research unit where experiments were conducted on bunnies and guinea pigs. I'm sure they weren't doing anything gruesome in there, but the threat to any research lab from the Animal Liberation Front was real and so the place was locked and alarmed.

I realised that I really had no good explanation for opening those doors so, as the porters arrived at high speed, I held up my hands and said sorry. I told them I had accidentally blunders into the wrong part of the building. It was stupid, but they didn't seem bothered at all. They turned the alarms off and left, and I never even thought about that lab again.

In 1989, while I was busy being an art student and piecing together my first fragments of the networks, an unknown researcher at a little-known science project in Europe was inventing a system to put hypertext on the networks. The researcher, an Englishman called Tim Berners-Lee, eventually came up with the name World Wide Web for his information system, but at the end of the eighties he was struggling to find a way to make it work. He later explained, 'Creating the web was really an act of desperation, because the situation without it was very difficult when I was working at CERN later. Most of the technology involved in the web, like the hypertext, like the internet, multifont text objects, had all been designed already. I just had to put them together.' When the project launched as a single website running out of his office it wasn't noticed by many. There were already a bunch of attempts to create graphical representations on the networks, and the Web looked like just another half-baked tool and nobody paid it much attention.

Although I hadn't heard of the Web, and I have no memory of when I first did come across it, I was very interested in hypertext systems alongside my growing interest in the networks. This interest was sparked initially by the Apple Mac Hypercard system which allowed you to create information systems of some complexity using a totally visual interface. In that way I was running alongside Berners-Lee in his search, although from a far inferior position. Berners-Lee himself didn't find his project plain sailing and he also encountered many doubters and mockers along the way. In his autobiography, Weaving the Web, he explained how he thought he could persuade one of the existing hypertext products to just add internet capability and this would solve everything.

'In September we went to the European Conference on Hypertext Technology (ECHT) at Versailles to pitch the idea. I approached Ian Ritchie and the folks from Owl Ltd, which had a product called Guide. The version now commercialised by Owl looked astonishingly like what I had envisioned for a Web browser — the program would open and display documents, and preferably let people edit them too. All that was missing was the Internet. *They've already done the difficult bit!* I thought, so I tried to persuade them to add an Internet connection. They were friendly enough, but they, too, were unconvinced.'

Every company that failed to grasp what he was talking about turned down potentially one of the greatest business opportunities of the century, but that doesn't surprise me at all. Almost nobody that I met was very interested in the internet. As Berners-

Lee says, 'people had to be able to grasp the Web in full, which meant imagining a whole world populated with Web sites and browsers. They had to sense the abstract information space that the Web could bring into being. It was a lot to ask.'

What did I know by the end of that time? Everything had changed and I felt I understood both art and the coming networks, but I didn't know where they would take me.

I wrote my graduation essay on computers, information and networks and called it The Art Of Networking. The work I made for my final show was much more traditional. I didn't use any of the things I'd discovered. I didn't use the big computer that I'd be offered, I fell back to the pure pleasure of construction, of found objects, industrial process, bricks, concrete, glass, canvas. I liked what I made but in retrospect I was falling back into a space that I knew well, and that I would continue to work in. My essay, on the other hand, gathered up a range of thoughts that were all my own.

It certainly wasn't a critical essay — it was more a piece of journalism, which prefigured things to come — but it got me out ahead of the crowd and forced me to examine the landscape for signs of movement. Not that anyone noticed and I was awarded an upper second, a 2:1.

As we graduated that year, mad things were happening outside college. In 1988, Mikhail Gorbachev had announced, in a speech at the United Nations, that the Soviet Union would no longer intervene in the affairs of its Eastern European satellite states. Those nations could now become democratic. It was the end of the Cold War and, as we reached the end of our art school years, the countries beyond the iron curtain started to rise up (or fall) like dominoes. The drama of those days affected us in strange ways. Some people jumped on trains and planes and went to see the fall of the Berlin wall. To this day I curse myself for my timidity, for not throwing everything to the wind and going to see history arrive.

I did notice how bulletin boards and online communications were being used during those revolutions to pass information and updates across the borders and this gave me a first understanding of how momentous the tools might be. I realised that finally there was a method of communication that routed around state control and put power into the hands of individuals. There were a lot of artists mixed up in the whole thing.

In my own life I was now firmly embedded in London, I understood the city. I had managed to get myself embedded and to survive, to put myself through college and to keep a relationship going. Most of my family had by now moved to the city as well, including my youngest brother, who was going to the London College of Printing to study photography. My partner had converted from teaching children to law and was entering that profession. My father had recovered well from his stroke and my parents had bought a small house in the south of France, my mother's dearest wish for years. The house provided an escape route that we took advantage of many times in those years as we all waited for something real, something concrete, to happen.

And then Margaret Thatcher was deposed as leader of the country and everything started to open up for the first time since the end of the seventies. It would take a few years, but the world was accelerating into this new era and we were along for the ride.

When we finally came to put on our graduation show, all the fight and fire had gone out of me. I was excited but already felt we were on the periphery of a jetstream that had gone off without us. I could see the art world in the distance but already I felt I didn't know how to connect with it, how to get its attention.

We put a good catalogue together, as good as they ever were. Again, black and white images and cryptic captions dominated. I tried to persuade everyone I knew to join me with a subversive act: to all use an image with a variation on a logo I had made on the Apple Mac with the slogan 'Goldsmiths 1990, Springboard to Success. Feed the hand that bites you.' Three others joined me, thus undermining their own promotion and engaging in egoless attitude. It was supposed to be close to meaningless, but not quite. The logos were superimposed on pages from a recruitment brochure. Mine showed a relay runner taking the baton and the headline, Teamwork, that's what wins in business. It was a KPMG advert. It was like I was warning myself; the world of business is out there; a baton is being passed. Ten years later I would come to know KPMG well, would spend a lot of time in those airless conference rooms that cost thousands in charged fees. For now, it all meant nothing. I was epatering the bourgeoisie.

John Thompson wrote a knowing introduction for us, failing to spot that the press was already in control of the narrative and were making rich heroes of a few.

    The Fine Art department here at Goldsmiths College is a place in which things never quite settle down. Like Platonic unrest, the dynamic of this state of positive instability is an ever-present reality, something to beg accepted and harnessed for the purpose of work rather than treated with suspicion and held at bay. Here, things can happen, things can change, they do happen and they do change. In terms of the kinds of things made, the issues which they address and the focus of the debate which surrounds them, things are always on the move. Of course, this is Goldsmiths viewed from the inside and presents a very different picture to that which its generally hawked by those in the media who choose to write about us, most of whom have never set foot in the place.

Our catalogue also contained a tribute to a student who had died during the course: Matthew Godwin, 1965-1989. I had briefly been friends with Ma hew in the early days of the course when we were based near Brixton. He was like me, a discoverer of interesting corners of the city and one day he came and told me there was a building nearby that contained a huge array of army surplus. There had been a fire and it was boarded up, but he had found out how to get in. I owned a van at the time and he asked if

I would be interested in collecting a couple of loads of this booty. I was interested but by the time we went to collect the treasure the entire building had been cleared. Matthew made some accusations, that I'd stolen his property, and we became less friends after that. I met him one more time, later that year in the early hours of the morning at a petrol station. He was with a young guy in a BMW, moving fast, living a life I couldn't imagine. And then he was gone.

Later there were more deaths from our cohort. Hamad Butt, who looked to be climbing the ladder of art with ease, was suddenly gone. And, later, another friend, Satu Krol. Two others climbed out of the mire to become true international art stars: Sam Taylor-Wood and Gillian Wearing. The rest of us went our separate ways and carved post art school lives out in that way that art students have, finding and refinding what it was that drove us, that made us artists. Others dropped away. A couple of years later I met someone from the year below me who had always seemed totally focussed on making art, on the art world. When I asked him how he was doing: he told me he was now a lawyer.

We put a great party together in a nightclub on the other side of the main road outside college. The day after we gathered, hungover, on the back field and drank beer. I wandered through the empty studios full of neatly laid out work. Nobody came after the families; nobody made the trip out to New Cross when Hirst wasn't there. I left all my work where it was when the show ended. I couldn't face dismantling the brick wall I had built, the concrete and drainpipe constructions. When someone asked me if I would put some work in a show I went back to collect some and found it had all been thrown out of the back door.

5

Beneath The Pavement, The Internet

My college days were over and suddenly that noisy dirty part of London seemed much less appealing. My partner found us a flat and we moved, to another dirty corner of London, to two floors, basement and ground, of a Victorian terraced house just behind a pedestrianised shopping street. We left New Cross and moved to Hackney.

I was twenty-nine and in a settled relationship which had sustained from my hometown, through her year of travelling around the world, my years of college and our move to Hackney. She was in the process of converting from teaching to becoming a lawyer. I had no qualifications, but the world seemed to be working to align itself with me. I didn't really know what to do to force that alignment. As always I didn't have a plan, but I had ideas and I had my epiphanies. I followed them blindly, not knowing where they would lead. I didn't look very far ahead. The aim was to make art and to satisfy my curiosity.

I had changed, I was in love with art and I was obsessed with networks. I had to work out what to do with this knowledge, though it didn't seem pressing, or even a concern. I just got on with things. I now had a right to do all the strange things that gave me pleasure. I had ways to explain them. I practised it in front of the mirror until I could say it with a straight face. 'My name is Ivan Pope and I am an artist.' It still felt like coming out, like admitting an addiction, that I'd fallen low but it really wasn't my fault. I professed a belief in a higher power. The cult was within me.

I had encountered the cult of the art world and I wasn't immune to its attractions, but it still seemed like a lottery, more like a game of chance than a career. Soon after my degree show I was contacted by someone who had a gallery, who wanted to put on a show. Excited, I went back to see what remained of the work I had abandoned in situ, but found it broken up and dumped out of the back door of the studio. It didn't matter, nothing came of the gallery. Being an ex-Goldsmiths student seemed to have some value but it was a volatile currency. Then there was the world of online. It was still mysterious to me, but I wondered whether there was a way of putting these two things together. The obvious approach was to make art with the networks. My moment of online epiphany remained with me. Although I still had little idea of the shape or form of the place, 'It's a real place, you could make work in there' still echoed within me.

The world itself had changed and was changing. Eastern Europe was in flux, Germany was unifying. Margaret Thatcher, a constant presence since my trip to Israel eleven years earlier, was gone by the end of the year. Nelson Mandela was released from prison in South Africa. The Yugoslavia that I had blithely hitchhiked through a few years before, now driven by the revived nationalisms unleashed by a restructuring Europe, started on the driven by the revived nationalisms unleashed by a restructuring Europe, started on the road to disintegration. The funny pleasure of a language called Serbo-Croat suddenly seemed to unbundle itself and presage a much darker world.

The UK plunged into ropey economic times as the ancient London that I had moved to so recently started to undergo a major transformation into a modern city. Damien Hirst's use of an empty building in the docks was not a chance occurrence, the dock lands were the site of a new gold rush. Thatcher had fired the starting gun for it, taking control of this vast empty but polluted in many ways land from the local Labour council and handing it over to her creation, the London Docklands Development Committee. My understanding of London had started on the Isle of Dogs at my sister's 'hard to let' flat in the seventies, at the end of the post war era. Now those docks that we had looked down into, which, hidden behind huge security walls had remained empty and unloved since the invention of containerisation and the moving of trade to bigger more modern ports, these spaces were to become the most valuable property in London.

Of course, artists were always the first to identify the opportunity of empty space and the docks were not terra nullis, empty land. There were occupants and had been from the start.

For his book, Hackney, That Rose-red Empire, the psychogeographic writer, Iain Sinclair, meandered at length through the past and present of the borough, assembling a portrait of a place in which he had lived for decades. Although written long after I had left, the world in the book is entirely identifiable as the Hackney we moved to.

Hackney, after all, is one of London's twilight zones, neither fish nor fowl. It's not North London, neither is it the East. It's by no means easy to get to. It has no tube, is poorly served by buses and its railway stations are on lines that link only to the hubs of other twilight zones.

We had moved away from the dirty streets of New Cross to the mean streets of Hackney, away from the main road which we thought of as a river which flowed ceaselessly day and night, and where we would be woken in the early hours by clusters of lorries on their way from the ferry. We moved away from the Hoffman presser and his charming smile and the ever-present smell of dry-cleaning fluid that permeated our flat in the summer. We left the streets with no green spaces and fled to Hackney, which, though poor had a middle-class centre that had its attractions. We rented two floors of a Victorian house from a Sri Lankan entrepreneur. It was in a short street of Victorian houses, right behind Marks and Spencers. I called it the middle-class zone and it felt safe enough yet remote enough for my life as an artist. As yet untouched by gentrification, at least in most parts, the vast borough represented a new start.

Hackney was perfect for me, perfect for us. It was a squatted marginal place full of dropped outs and the excluded with huge council estates but also a culture of resistance. There were no coffee shops anywhere at that point, certainly not in our new part of town. Nobody considered it a valuable place to live, but even a short walk around the neighbourhood revealed to me that it was filled with splendid decaying buildings, Georgian houses, squares, factories, alleyways, churches, even a National Trust house, the not very grand but ours all the same Sutton House, at the time half derelict and prone to the depredations of passing squatters and thieves.

On the first weekend at our new house, I popped out on the Saturday morning to get a newspaper. I had lived near here when I was first in London, on Lower Clapton Road, which at the time was being called Murder Mile by the local papers. There was a fair amount of violence around and a man had been found dead in his flat soon after Greg had moved there. We often laughed about it. The only people who really moved to Hackney in those days were people looking for heap accommodation and squatters — and possibly gangsters. The estates just up the road from us had a fearsome reputation for gangs but were also heavily squatted. The days of short life housing and tolerated squatting were long gone but the era of trendy Hackney and huge house prices weren't foreseen. Hackney was something of an oasis, isolated from the centre of London but not that far from it. It was also full of artists and students and you could score decent drugs in the pubs. At the top of the road a huge pub had just been re-opened after an enforced police closure and was offering an upwardly mobile menu that was a novelty in the area.

Now we'd moved back I wasn't really clear where anything was and so I went out onto the main road where I thought there was a newspaper shop. Pretty quiet around here, I thought, comparing it to the noisy chaos of New Cross. I bought my paper and was about to turn back off the road when I noticed a car come around the corner at the bottom of Mare Street. That one is going a bit fast, I thought, and as this thought entered my head, Hackney exploded into noise and chaos all of its own. As I focused on the speeding car I became aware of the sounds of police sirens and then, as if in a movie, two police cars shot around the corner in pursuit. My mouth dropped open as, right in front of me, the original car smashed into an oncoming vehicle, span around, wheels falling off, doors flying open. As the car came to a halt, as if by magic more police cars arrived from the other direction, policemen flying out of them and diving on top of the car driver who had fallen out through his open door.

Within moments a sleepy Saturday morning scene had been converted in total mayhem. I looked at the car that had been struck and noticed that it had a family in it but nobody was paying it any attention. I went over and pulled the driver's door open and asked if they were alright. They sat there in bemused silence, their wrecked car emitting steam. I told them they had better get out. By then ambulances, more police vehicles and hundreds of members of the public had converged on the scene. A man sat handcuffed on the road and a clean-up operation swung into action. I decided I had seen enough, so I tucked my newspaper under my arm and went home, with the phrase, 'You'll never believe what just happened' forming on my lips.

Why did we move to Hackney, to the bottom end of Mare Street where a tiny middle-class enclave sheltered behind Marks and

Spencers. It was a random decision stemming from a small advert of a flat to let, but we were fed up with New Cross and there was nothing to keep us in that desert. I was broke. We upped and left and discovered a new world and, although we were only just down the road from Upper Clapton Road where I had spent time with Greg in the flat above the launderette, it didn't seem connected. The world had changed, I was changed. The Narroway, on which Jack Cohen had opened his first Tesco bank account, almost linked those two worlds, also divided my new home from the wastes of that road, from the murder mile.

Of course, the transition was not as sharp as that. The roads above the Narroway led only slowly to the suburbs, to Hackney Marshes and outwards to the M11 and the outer reaches. Yet, there seemed to be a change and, after moving to Brett Road, we seldom ventured beyond our little shopping street - except after falling asleep on a night bus, when I might find myself walking back from the very edges of civilisation. The actual borough was huge, it stretched all the way down to gentrified Islington in the south and northwards and east. I never discovered the boundaries because the Hackneyness seemed to dissolve when you got away from Mare street. Further up Amherst Road were huge estates of council flats filled with anarchist squatters and the driving force behind Class War, who were at that time epatering the bourgeoisie. But Hackney was perfect for the next part of my life. It offered room to grow, room to stretch. It was terra nullis in many ways yet it was also full of artists and studios and galleries. Between my new flat and the tied up tight centre of London was Shoreditch, an indistinct corner on a busy through road that was about to become the epicentre of a new art world.

For a few months we sat in our Eastern fastness and brooded.

In the little yard at the back of our new flat was a wisteria plant that grew, Jack and the Beanstalk style, up a brick wall and into the sky. Along the top of the wall was a line of windows. The building stretched along all the backs of the houses in both directions.

Intrigued, I left the house and walked down the street to an alley and found, wedged in between three streets as if it had been lowered from a helicopter, a triangular concrete and brick building with old fashioned industrial doors, metal grills on the windows. At one end above a much larger entrance, a carved stone sign which said, simply, Temple Works.

It may or may not have had an estate agent's board on it, I can't remember, but it looked empty, abandoned and tempting. I told my cousin about it and we came back later that night with some tools and quickly broke in. Climbing the concrete staircase, we stopped at the first floor where a pair of locked factory doors barred our way. There was a hole broken in them, someone else had been here before us. I shone a torch through and peeked in. Behind me Greg, eager to know what was in there, asked what I saw. I couldn't resist echoing Howard Carter on peering into the tomb of Tutankhamun. 'Wonderful things', I replied.

I had to find some sort of job, if not a career. I still wasn't very interested in either. I should have been probing the art world, but my experience of Goldsmiths had got me interested in computers and networks, desk top publishing and, although I was still making work and fascinated by the art world, I was excited by the new worlds I had opened up. I wanted to make art, but I didn't really understand the system and didn't feel up to finding out. My inability to be clubbable probably kept me away from the action because, although I went to a lot of openings and artist parties, I would usually end up standing in a corner drinking myself into a stupor or just idly chatting to the few people I knew in the scene. This was the moment when I should have been pushing for connections, furiously networking, bouncing off my gold-plated Goldsmiths connections. Instead, I sat in my cavernous free studio in the backwater of Hackney and daydreamed about computer networks and magazines.

I also really needed a job and was given a lead by Rachel from Goldsmiths. She had been the publisher of the Spotlight newsletter and my co-pilot in learning desk top publishing. She had graduated a year ahead of me and spent some time in what she called the most awful job, laying out catalogues for a fat ex-banker in an office in Victoria. She told me she was giving it up and warned me that it wasn't much of an opportunity. Don't take it full time, she said, and make sure you get your money each week. I mostly ignored her advice. I was still obsessed with desk top publishing and thought I should be able to earn a living from the hard-won skills I had picked up at college. There didn't seem to be any jobs for Ventura experts though so I grabbed at what I could get and took the job.

The company collected publicly available information about electronic trading systems and collated it into fat catalogues, which I laid out. The catalogues were printed and sent out, unrequested, with an invoice. The basic premise was that a certain percentage of big companies would just pay what was an inflated but not outrageous amount without asking who had actually ordered the thing. However, some got extremely agitated and would phone repeatedly to make their point. The office, above a shop in a backstreet in Victoria, was a horrible hole, the editor a strange, etiolated lecher in a bad wig. Everyone ate takeaways at their desks and left deposits of grime. There were no cleaners.

Bailiffs turned up regularly and tried to take the computers away. We were instructed not to let them in, which meant that we could often not get in ourselves. Salaries came in strange ways and intermittently, despite Rachel's warnings. One time the boss flew to Europe and came back with a vast wedge of pound notes which he doled out in the back office. Reminding me of Billy Bunter and his postal order, he endlessly claimed he was about to get a huge payoff from his previous firm for some amazing deal he had put together involving Arabian princes and American oil barons, but it never transpired.

Despite all of that, a good thing about the job was being in the city as a worker, a new experience for me. I used to go and get a toasted bagel or pop into a new sandwich bar that seemed like something made in heaven. It was the second branch of Pret a Manger and a harbinger of a new world. I also learnt a lot, although I didn't realise it for years, about the bluster needed to run a failing business when things got tricky. I don't know what happened to that man, or to that company, but a whole new world was coming that would blow them away.

My cousin called and told me he was going to Glasgow to do a film event at the National Review of Live Art. Did I want to go along and help out? Of course I did. We set out a week later in a borrowed car loaded with projectors and sheets, stopping only to collect another friend on the way, a skilled musical hippy called Tim. We drove nonstop to Glasgow, taking it in turns to steer the ancient Ford which seemed to slither and slide around on the road, although that might have been due to the amount of dope we smoked as we drove.

The next day we were shown our working space, on Renfrew Street, in the basement of an industrial building at the bottom of a hill. It was accessed through a community space that included rehearsal studios, but the space itself seemed separate from the world, a dark place in the bowels of the building. All of this influenced us as we set about building an event from scratch, with only Greg's internal vision to guide us. He had hand made hundreds of feet of film working directly on clear 16mm stock using ink, Letraset rub-down transfers and masking tape. In this way he created films very cheaply.

Our show was called Effects of Darkened Rooms. The space they had found for us was wonderful and really suggested the show, even Loophole itself, to us. It was site specific at its best, the fusion of event and location. Obviously, we'd never done it before, we'd never even worked together before, but over the next two days we rigged curtains, power, projectors and lighting and conjured an experience out of very little. Tim tootled on various wind instruments as a plan came together. We designed the space in three sections. First we constructed the shadow screen, which we stretched floor to ceiling opposite the entrance. This enclosed the audience in a tight space at the start of the event, they had no idea of the lay-out of the basement and we wished to reveal the architecture to them in a slow procession. Behind the shadow screen we constructed a framework with lengths of timber and metal recovered from builders skips in the surrounding streets. This installation would cast its shadows as well as our own onto the screen, it also worked as a percussive instrument – we came armed with drumsticks to effect a soundtrack to this section of the event.

In the evenings we went out drinking with the festival crowd. Each morning we returned to our basement with a hangover. The basement closed in on us. We constructed an alternate world. We had no idea how or if it would work, it was done on instinct. We didn't even know if anyone would make the trip to see the show.

I don't even remember whether we did the show more than once. It feels like it was one perfect moment. We had no notion of managing the event, we just aimed to fire it off and hope for the best. The venue had an entrance that led off the street down a huge wide staircase which was like descending into some infernal depths. On the first night when we opened the doors a sizable crowd flooded down the stairs and filled the first space. We shut the doors, hermetically sealing the space. Anyone prone to panic in dark spaces would panic now. We did whatever it was we did in the first space. We turned on lights in the second space and learnt a great lesson: audiences are like sheep and you can control them with light. Tim made ethereal noises on an ancient clarinet. The audience drifted lost through a grey world, confused and amazed, enfolded within our creation. We took them on a short loop around the space, but they all thought they had been through a huge maze. We knew we'd done something special and that there was a lot of potential in the Loophole effect.

To our amazement the whole thing worked. The audience was appreciative, and audience numbers grew with every performance. We realised we were doing something which intrigued people. It wasn't proper live art, it wasn't a proper film and it wasn't a proper installation. It managed to fall between all the art stools. As the people perused this new environment, we quietly exited and left them to it. We turned to each other and asked 'how's it supposed to end?' and 'how will they know when to go?' We decided to give no sign and leave this last part running as a final installation, a policy we adopted for many subsequent shows. It meant in a way that the 'thing' never ended, anyone could stay or not and it left the whole action open-ended and unresolved.

We left Glasgow a few days later in the same red waggon. A huge and encompassing rainstorm engulfed us as we climbed over the mountains, leaving me in fear for my life as we overtook endless lorries. Further south, Greg filmed the long evening shadows as we passed outside Lockerbie. We had learnt some great lessons about how an audience would respond to work and that we could build things from scratch in a short time. We'd also seen something very important about our work, that it could happen anywhere, in any type of space.

Over the next few years we put these lessons to good and bad use, culminating in a show in a vast empty steelworks in the Ruhr Valley, where the tricks learnt on that first night of bricolage came into their own. Loophole could only hold together by actively moving on. Every show took us somewhere new. I now had two streams of thought to contend with: the creative joy of putting on a show with an actual audience who liked it and the potential that computers and networks offered, but which nobody could see yet. I didn't realise I had to make a decision on which to go for. I thought I could merge them seamlessly.

After we got home from Glasgow we discussed the thing we'd invented, which we called the Shadow Engine, and where we might go next. Greg suggested doing something in the basement at the Filmmakers' Co-op. I decided to quit my awful job and, happy to be broke, took up residence in Temple Works which I regarded as my own studio. London was full of empty buildings in those days. There was a property slump on, a recession, and nobody wanted the old bits of the city. Banks had repossessed thousands of properties that had been used to secure loans, but there were no tenants to be had. The dynamics that had led to Damien Hirst's show in Docklands didn't extend as far as Hackney where there was no eager Thatcherite authority ready to throw money at the problem. The building I had occupied was hidden in a backstreet, the detritus of the rag trade that had historically employed large swathes of the local workforce. Now it was redundant and surplus to requirements, and nobody would even come to have a look at what they owned for the next few years. The space was incredible, a triangular concrete framed building that fitted precisely into the triangle left by gardens and the alleyway.

The building was full of material, patterns, cutting tables and equipment. It looked like the workforce had got up one day and walked out and never come back, which they probably had. There were newspaper pages and rude graffiti, personal belongings and half made clothing, business cards and huge scissors. The middle floor had large windows along one side which let out onto the flat roof of part of the ground floor. Somebody had broken in through these windows only to deposit a lot of garden waste in the space. It was clear that feral cats had taken up residence and we found the mummified remains of one in the corner. At first I walked around taking photos of the objects, but we soon took to clearing and dismantling the bigger tables. Scattered throughout the floors were many wooden and industrial stools, beautiful objects in their own right which I still come across in friends' houses to this day.

I went back to my own project and spent six months through a freezing winter into the beginning of 1991 building an installation in the factory while popping up and down to Newport to teach art and technology for Roy Ascott. I worked on my own in semidarkness, slowly dismantling the huge cutting tables and clearing the space, then bringing in various materials, some from the upper floors, which were lighter and brighter — they had windows. I discovered that there was power available on the upper floor and I ran extensions down. Finally, I had light and stopped being quite so fearful of the dark corners where I was working. I did find that I enjoyed working on my own though. I was happy to be alone for long stretches, and my huge installation slowly grew into

Temple Works was big enough to absorb other artists and as it got cleaned up, emptied out and the water and electricity sorted out, so more people started moving in to use the floors. I kept a tight rein on the top floor and the ground floor though. I was building an installation on the ground floor and the top floor became a workshop for myself and Loophole Cinema. Through the cold winter I worked away until finally I was done. At the start of the following year I called the installation In Mourning for Nothing and threw it open to the world. It was advertised in Time Out and I had some cards printed up, but Hackney was the back of beyond and after a riotous opening night party there were few visitors. I did get my first review, in a radical leftist magazine. It was written by the mother of my friend Bea, who had joined Loophole Cinema. It was the only art review I would ever get.

Altared Images, Temple Works

Something different is coming out of Goldsmiths school of art, better known for turning out marketable young formalists for West End galleries.

Anyone who knew the Arts Lab back in the sixties would feel a sense of familiarity about the Temple Works in Hackney. A group of ex-Goldsmiths students (to be distinguished emphatically from the 'Freeze' group on whom media interest focused a while back) have squatted this derelict factory and aim to present 'non-categorisable work', including film and installations, 'mixing freely' in a context 'accessible to everyone'.

Ivan Pope specifies how their aims differ from the better known Goldsmiths groups: 'They're on the margins trying to enter the art scene; we're not interested in promoting personalities.' Pope, using found objects, demands the participation of an audience forced either to view his work through voyeurs' peepholes or be viewed on the outside of it. He insists on his right to a fluidity that places him outside the market. This piece is part of his current year of installations, which is in progress and will continue after the public show : less work-of-art than art-at-work.

Sean Loughrey's highly catholic venues for a series of on-site projections include a demolished hotel, a renovated yacht club, Hadleigh Castle and the Elephant and Castle shopping centre.

MAVIS HAUT, CATALYST MAGAZINE

6

The Matrix

1991

Commercial Internet eXchange (CIX) Association, Inc. formed

Wide Area Information Servers (WAIS), invented by Brewster Kahle, released by Thinking Machines Corporation

Gopher released by Paul Lindner and Mark P. McCahill from the Univ of Minnesota

World-Wide Web (WWW) released by CERN; Tim Berners-Lee developer. First Web server is nxoc01.cern.ch, launched in Nov 1990 and later renamed info.cern.ch.

PGP (Pretty Good Privacy) released by Philip Zimmerman

NSFNET traffic passes 1 trillion bytes/month and 10 billion packets/month

RFC 1216: Gigabit Network Economics and Paradigm Shifts

RFC 1217: Memo from the Consortium for Slow Commotion Research (CSCR)

Countries connecting to NSFNET: Croatia (HR), Hong Kong (HK), Hungary (HU), Poland (PL), Portugal (PT), Singapore (SG), South Africa (ZA), Taiwan (TW), Tunisia (TN)

[HOBBES' INTERNET TIMELINE]

Desperate to continue work with networks I looked around at what was going on elsewhere and came across things called Bulletin Boards (BBS). They looked like a lesser, toy version of the Internet, but as I read about them, I started to lust after them. They seemed like a tool that had grown from grass roots and which I should be able to work out for myself. The BBS software reminded me of desk-top publishing. It put the means of communication in the hands of the user.

Bulletin boards were services run on ordinary PCs. There was commercial software available, which I could run on my own PC. Users would dial up to them using a phone line and a modem connected to their computer to log on. What fascinated me about them was that they seemed to replicate magazines, they were all about content and communities, two things that had always interested me.

It was like desktop publishing all over again. The lure of putting together a magazine with the content I wanted, and then making it available to others, was exciting. There was a thriving bulletin board scene in America with some very successful commercial boards. Even better, groups of boards had banded together and created bigger networks so that in theory you could access a sort of mini internet from the first board. The best thing about all of this to me was that others had already done the hard work and I could buy into it.

I already knew that I wasn't going to be a programmer, I would never write any software. My interest had started to coagulate around the content, the publishing element of networks. Although it seems obvious in retrospect, it wasn't articulated at the time— without content, all the networks were nothing. The existing academic and commercial networks didn't notice this be-cause they took it for granted that their networks contained the content they wanted to see. Only in the world of bulletin boards and a few other communities (such as The Well in California and CIX in the UK) were entrepreneurial types learning how to at-tract and keep audiences.

I found an American magazine called Boardwatch, a sort of fanzine for bulletin boards. It had a money-making attitude, it stressed how you could make your board successful, what hard-ware and software were available. I read it in rapt fascination and decided that this was a publishing medium for me. Without even realising it I had found a new publishing mode which rang all my bells.

In a state of excitement and typical eager over excitement (dosed liberally with bullshit), I invented my own bulletin board and ap-plied for a grant from the Arts Council. It was duly granted. I suggested I was going to set up and run an experimental bulletin board for artists. I was still running art and networks in parallel. I called it Artnet and after I got the grant I set about building it on a cheap PC that I got from Morgans in New Oxford Street, the home of cheap computer kit. My bulletin board ran slap bang into Metcalfe's law, although I didn't know then that it existed. This law states that the effect of a telecommunications network is proportional to the square of the number of connected users of the system. For example, when there is only one fax machine in the world it has no value but adding one more machine gives it value. Each new machine that joins the network adds more value than a single extra user because everyone benefits. This is a network effect. The same applies to computer networks.

In my case the number of connected users never rose much above three, thus both proving Metcalf and disproving all my enthusiasms. This fundamental description of the value of networks is a sort of law for early adopters, for those who are so damned smart that they invent things before they can become a reality. It is also a huge warning flag: if you don't get the numbers you don't succeed. Artnet came nowhere near succeeding, it didn't even flare briefly, but it taught me a lot about putting stuff together, and I noticed that although nobody used it, everybody was really interested. I became a pathfinder, someone who tried out new things only to watch them snatched away by harder nosed, better organised people - or just those with a bit more staying power. It is often said that the bleeding edge is where you really bleed, and I did a lot of bleeding. But only at the edge do you get to see new things emerge from the mud.

By April 1992 we had been living in Margaret Thatcher's world since we were teenagers and it seemed we were due for a change. That year we sat up late on election night at my friend's flat where I'd lived as a student, waiting for the expected Labour victory, only to be devastated as it became clear that the Conservatives had won again, this time under the grey man, John Major. Thatcher was gone but still there was no change of government.

Yugoslavia had started to break up, setting in train years of ethnic cleansing and the sort of murderous European war that we thought was long gone. For the rest of the year, while the European Union was bringing itself into being with the ratification of the Maastricht Treaty, the disintegration of Yugoslavia continued remorselessly. In the United States, sales of CDs overtook those of cassettes for the first time. Our future was arriving but it was very unevenly distributed.

The Internet was rumbling along under the ground, below the viewpoint and understanding of most people, growing and stretching out its tentacles to draw in more and more culture.

The networks started to make more demands on me. To those, and there were many, who already had a toehold, it seemed like a jolly private club, a place where one made friends and cha ed to them out of the view of mortals. Apart from the academic denizens, who mostly though not exclusively, had academic interests, and the small commercial world, who got access because they were somehow connected to the academics, there were various islets of commercial users, an archipelago of connectedness.

I found a book, John S. Quaterman's The Matrix: Computer Networks and Conferencing Systems Worldwide, which held out huge promise. It seemed like a skeleton key to the world of networks. I wasn't technically literate enough to make use of the detail, but it was very exciting. I felt I had bought an atlas from a lost world, huge and dense and filled with maps and a strange language that I never quite came to understand.

There was CIX and The Well and Compuserve and Delphi and many other commercial services, and there were dozens of tiny pools of online talent. There were actually hundreds, if not thousands, of networks around the world, an archipelago of half-connected networks, big and small. The complex mesh of different closed and commercial networks, the gateways and protocols, the acronyms: NORDUnet, DREnet, EUnet, UUCP, BITNET, EARN, HEPnet, JANET, all of this is unknown to today's users of the internet.

" *In your hands you hold a window to the world. This is a travelogue for anyone, whether you're a free-spirited network pioneer whose login sessions include trips around the world, a novice computer user who is just embarking on a new journey, or a researcher who collaborates with colleagues.' I was all of those things.*

Departure is at any time from any place and you can return whenever you want. You set the time, you set the pace. You have the freedom to explore and discover as you please. The only limit is your imagination.

It was like being handed a travel guide to a land where nobody I knew had been. It made me realise that what I was looking at wasn't a technical space, it was a human space, an art space, a place for everyone. Quartarman took some effort to look at the world that he knew was arriving, referring to some science fiction that had anticipated these networks.

In 1980, a science fiction writer noticed an interesting property of computer aided interaction and wrote a story about it called "True Names!. He noticed that computer users can sometimes masquerade under false identities and defeat attempts to determine who they are: this was well known to system administrators, but Vernor Vinge was apparently the first to turn it into fiction. Quarterman had another even more chilling insight.

But most of the best of fiction concerning computer networks is also concerned with other aspects of identity. One of the clearest explanations of the political use of personae created by means of computer networks is Ender's Game by Orson Scott Card. It involves invented characters who expound on political theory in order to influence public opinion and elections. This idea has been ridiculed by some writers, but there are contemporary parallels.

He foresaw and touched on many issues that were to come into close focus in the decades that followed: etiquette, ethics, legality. The world he sketched out is now almost unrecognisable: it is a moment in history that has gone. He was writing even before the fall of the Soviet empire and he pointed out that the Eastern block was not really connected to the networks, nor was South Africa in the time before the end of apartheid.

Much of the book beyond the foreword never made much sense to me but it changed my view of everything and led to the adventures that followed. I saw it as a futuristic guide to an unknown world with maps and connections. There were empty lands, dangerous zones and even 'Here be Monsters'. I was hooked, but first I had to find a way to get into the actual internet, whatever it was composed of.

Desperate to find some sort of work, I went back to see my friends in Goldsmiths Computer Centre, my first visit since graduating. I needed to print out my dissertation: I thought my final year essay might be useful in helping me find a job. I went to see Wendy, the centre secretary, who knew everything and who had always been kind to me when I was a student. When I poked my head around her office door the first thing she said was, 'Have you come about the job?'. I didn't know what she meant.

'We've got a new job going, it's your job! You have to apply.'

She handed me a form. 'There's a week left to apply.'

I didn't think I qualified, but I decided to have a punt, guessing I had nothing to lose. I missed the college environment and the computers and I needed a job. I knew everyone there and liked them. Best of all it would give me access to the networks that I was still obsessed with. Not the internet, even they didn't have that yet, but it would be a start. Proper internet access was more likely to arrive at a university computer centre than at home. It couldn't be long before they got it, I thought. A week later, on the last day for applications, as a snowstorm closed down the city and the transport system collapsed into chaos, I made my way across a desolate London from Hackney to New Cross and hand delivered my application.

They invited me for an interview and I arrived to find the interview panel chaired by the Fine Art Bigwig himself, the Dean of Arts, Peter Cresswell. He obviously didn't know my part in the drama which led to his appearance on the front page of the Sun and he was friendly. It must have come as a pleasant surprise to be greeted by someone that he had a chance of understanding. I was determined to drive that advantage home. It was my only solid card. I had proved myself by working in the computer department. My dissertation was on point. I had run a bulletin board for artists, that must have made me pretty unique despite having no users. I had a lot to say about what computers and students should get up to together, while being careful not to obsess over the Internet itself.

I realised that once I got an interview I was pretty convincing and could close the deal. Maybe the novelty of having an actual fine art student apply for a job with them added some luster. I have no idea what they asked me, but I know I sketched out a vision of computers as central to the college's mission. As the computer centre was still working out of the science labs with the sinks and teak work surfaces and even fold up Bunsen burners, I guess they saw something of the future, someone who understood what was coming down the tracks.

I let them have my vision, such as it was, full on. I didn't know much technical stuff about computers but I always had a vision, which was that access to computing should be spread a lot further around the campus. That seemed obvious. After all, I had been the first art faculty member to crack the system, and here I was applying for job to pass on what I'd learnt. What could go wrong?

As I got home the phone rang and they offered me the job. On May 1st a letter came confirming it. I became a Programmer Advisor on £2,086 a month plus London Weighting. My stated role included provision of programming advice to academic and administrative computer users, the development, documentation and support of specific software projects, installing and configuring software throughout the college, developing expertise and running introductory courses, provision of systems support and liaison with suppliers. There was no mention of the internet, which was really the only reason I was going back. No matter, I was sure I would soon have the entire college on the networks.

It was the first real job I ever got, and more or less the last.

Suddenly I was back working in the computer centre. I moved onto the campus. The lab itself hadn't changed much since I had left. It was still furnished with the chemistry benches from its previous existence. If you lifted the lids around the benches you would find laboratory sinks complete with fold down taps and gas taps. I liked to show these to unsuspecting students and staff. Some new PCs lined the benches, but they still had no connectivity to each other: there were no networks and certainly no internet. It was like a place that Borges might describe, or Orwell, a mix of the modern and the redundant, perhaps the Soviet Union had similar setups. For me it was the normal order of things, but I was determined to change it. There were many dumb terminals, linked to a central micro-computer running VAX-VMS which were used for student number crunching. This was considered a really clever machine and was guarded by a priesthood to which I was not admitted.

I became the Apple Mac guru as none of the existing staff thought those machines were worth their attention. They had acquired one of the new colour Macs with a decent sized monitor and this was given to me as my personal machine. I felt like a millionaire. Not only was I earning more money than I had ever earned, which wasn't difficult, I had access to all the computers I wanted and the prestige of a serious job at a quality institution. I advised the users of the college's computers, a fast-growing area. PCs started to flood the college, PCs running DOS, a text interface that was the norm at the time. For students, we offered mainly WordPerfect, the world's most successful word processing program at the time. There were no mice and no graphical user interface for the program. For all that, it was fairly complex and I became a wizard with WordPerfect and DOS – the first and last time I was to feel in control of any technology.

At first we staff shared one large office. It was terrible. There was no privacy and we got on each other's nerves. I sat in the corner with my Mac feeling lost, in their world. The job was great, there were a lot of art students and some interesting projects and for a while the drama of new possibilities made me forget about the lack of Internet connections. Colour printers and multimedia kit started to arrive. We even built a network for sorts, a Novell network that was supposed to link all the PCs. It was made out of a lovely cabling system called thin Ethernet that joined together at the ends with bayonet fitting connectors. The same cabling worked for video and I soon realised it had a lot of uses outside the institution. I was forever liberating parts from the store for art projects.

I was still part of Loophole Cinema which wasn't going to go away just because I had a job. Greg found us a gig at the London Filmmakers Co-op where he was now hanging out and working. The co-op was a leftover from the seventies, an alternative organisation based in an old railway building alongside the vast marshalling yards behind Camden. The building had once been a laundry and while the upstairs contained the offices, workshops and a small cinema for filmic events to take place, there was also a cold echoing basement underneath, reached down a metal staircase. This space was suggested for a Loophole event and we took to it eagerly, partly because it took us to the heart of our culture and partly because it was free and accessible.

We moved in as before with piles of materials, projectors and films and no real idea of what we were going to do. Through a process of experimentation and elimination we built a fabric maze from rolls of lining material that Temple Works provided. This was a more considered environment. Visitors entered the maze, created with material stretched at head height onto which films were projected. Although it wasn't much of a maze, we realised that people allowed themselves to be trapped in it due to the disorientating effect of the films as they stretched and elongated along the surfaces.

In a side room we constructed a terrifying machine from a pair of old fans and a projector, all chained together and hanging from the ceiling. The device projected one of Greg's abstract hand made films onto the wall, a bonus being that it also transmitted a horrendous audio track. This emerged from the optical sound reader converting the edge of the film into sound. The effect seemed to be a parody of black and white films of the first world war, all exploding bombs and spraying mud in a blasted landscape of barbed wire and death. It reminded me of my piece for my Foundation graduation a few years before, Slow Death, but with a more violent noise. It's commonplace to say that nobody would be allowed to get away with such dangerous events nowadays, but it seems true - much of our stuff was lethal, even before we became interested in Mark Pauline and his Survival Research Laboratories. Everybody on the circuit that we now started to engage with flirted with extreme sound and extreme danger. It was only going to get worse.

Soon after I started at Goldsmiths I came across a new Arts Council fund, the New Collaborations Fund, which seemed tailor made for Loophole. It was 'to support the development of inter-disciplinary work and emerging new multi-disciplinary art forms'.

The Shadow Engine has its base in interactive film, I wrote. *Loophole Cinema now wishes to move this base towards the use of computer-generated imagery and computer control mechanisms. The intention is to create work that is interactive, multi-disciplinary and innovative. To this end we are proposing a research programme with two strands.* Essentially the research is to discover whether it is possible for us to move away from more 'traditional' art use of film, sound and structure towards a total interactive shadow environment. I thought that the mix of Loophole Cinema's analogue madness and my interest in digital creation should be what they were looking for, and I was right. Using my new office as a base I put in an application and we were awarded a grant of just over four thousand pounds, a fortune to us at that time. I didn't consult with Greg or any of the Loophole crew, I just invented a research and development project for Loophole's Shadow Engine and they gave us the money.

We were invited back to the Filmmakers Co-op for the 1991 London Film Festival that October. We had been working hard in Temple Works in the interim and for the festival we debuted our Propaganda Beacons.

The Propaganda Beacons were like the lovechild of an arc welder and a Dansette record player crossed with a piles of scrap steel and sheet glass. We spent long nights in the studio building structures to hold working record players. We placed a pierced metal tube directly on the vinyl and hung a light bulb inside it. When the records turned the light emitted shaped rays from the tube while the needle, stuck in a groove, repeated a loop of sound. The light reflected in the glass panes. After we had built two or three of these towers and tested them we realised we'd made something eerie. The combined light and soft sounds combined to build an illusory world that had the capacity to scare us by whispering in our ears.

We took five or six of these machines to the Filmmakers and showed our Propaganda Beacons piece there. Inside the avant-garde space that allowed us to make these simple yet complex works there was no technology at all, or at least nothing recognisable of the world that was emerging. Everything had been invented at the end of the Victorian age, projectors, film, lights, theatre, illusion, optics. Yet outside that world I returned to a fast-moving new age where information flew down wires and images were conjured on computer screens.

The move to Hackney for me had opened up a variety of new parts of London. I'd always been drawn to the industrial, to inner city decay and the possibility of treasure from trash. My whole introduction to London had been by way of a derelict Isle of Dogs and then on to Brick Lane. My sister had taken me there in the late seventies, to eat at the Aladdin or the Nazrul, the first curry houses on what was at that point a poor inner-city district with a growing population of Bengali and Pakistani immigrants looking for a better life. The fabric of the buildings was awful. The previous Jewish population had moved out between the fifties and the seventies but the Great Synagogue was still there, it had not yet become the Mosque.

Hackney yielded up Temple Works, and many more interesting buildings, all the way up Mare Street towards Bethnal Green. East of where we lived wasn't so interesting. Property prices and thus rents were still low and anyway, nobody was really assessing areas for their value. There were rich pickings for artists, spaces to work, to show work, to gather and make a noise, make a mess. And there was history.

Dalston, with its market and clubs, sat just to the West of us, within walkable distance. Greg introduced me to the place with a lock in at the Pembury pub and it became a regular place to visit for shopping and, in the watches of the night, for bagels and coffee. A bagel shop on the market stayed open twenty-four hours and, in an era before coffee shops, before Uber, before night tubes, we tended to share taxis around the dark city, or walk long distances. We would visit the shop at Dalston market in the early hours of the morning and share the premises with clubbers, punks, junkies, police and thieves. It was neutral territory and the food was great.

Further west lay Shoreditch, a similarly abandoned part of London which housed a variety of dodgy pubs, clubs and kebab houses, but few signs of culture. We hung out around Hoxton Square, which was a collection of industrial buildings which had seen better days. On the corner a huge empty industrial site was taken over by the circus school. My friend Bea's boyfriend Gavin had rented the top floors of an old printing works. The area was changing, artists were moving in fast and the old industrial buildings were being converted into studios, but it was still a mostly unwanted and unloved part of London, beyond the pale to everyone except the outcasts and the artists. It was always the artists who started the process of bringing the wasteland back into use. Hoxton Square was not yet the centre of the art world that it was to become, but the creatives were gathering. We recognised the opportunity, the cheap buildings, the distance from the centre, the space to expand.

The 1990s will hold new approaches to interpretation. The absence of matter in the making of images, and the complexity with which time and space are constructed, fulfil the earliest calls for the 'total' artwork by artists earlier in the century, which include Lissitsky, Kandinsky and Artaud.

In November I launched an email Newsletter about art, inspired by other online art Newsletter s that I'd come across. I had two art mailing lists as well, Artnet and Art-support, both run out of an educational resource in Newcastle. I was getting tugged into the undertow of creativity and my approach was to hunt down everything, approach it from all sides. There wasn't much going on online, so I started to look at real world events. There wasn't much computer art, so I invented a way of bringing a lot of other stuff into the mix. I wasn't really aware of it, but I was desperate to publish, to construct that mix of knowledge and control that I loved in magazines. Deep down inside I knew that this was what the internet was for, and that I was searching for it with bulletin boards and email Newsletter s and everything else. But it was going to take some time to arrive.

I set out my manifesto for the first issue.

> *I have taken the title of Also Known As Art for this on-line publication because I believe that there are countless things that we can DECIDE TO KNOW AS ART. Art should not begin and end with 'artists'. I am interested in how non-art areas and activities can be discovered, assessed and brought within the ambit of 'art'.*
> *This can only be good for us all.*

I wrote a piece about one of my obsessions at the time, the idea that there should be an electronic version of the Filmmakers Co-op, hoping that we could form this, that we were on the edge of a new revolution, that the nineties might be like the sixties again, bringing new forms of art. I proposed the founding of 'a new artists' co-operative. The London Electronic Media Co-op would provide access to the new electronic media.' I showed my evident frustration with technology. 'Technology is generally guarded by a 'priesthood' of technicians who refuse to let their power be diluted by 'mere artists'.' Anna Couey sent me copies of Arts Wire News from San Francisco. Arts Wire, started by Anne Foucke, was like Artnet though they hadn't got online yet. I also got a flyer from an organisation in California called Art Com, who had formed the Art Com Electronic Network (ACEN). They held out the potential of electronic art galleries, art information databases, periodicals and even an electronic shopping mall. They were based on The Well, a Californian bulletin board that for a brief moment seemed to be the centre of the online universe. I realised that there were others in my space, and lots of them were in advance of my rudimentary progress.

In my role of computer centre advisor, I went on a visit to Kings College in the University of London to see the real internet at work. The person who was demonstrating this real internet interface used an Apple greyscale monitor with a graphical interface. He showed me a seemingly endless listing on a server somewhere on the other side of the world. 'This is where you get software', he said. I stared at the screen, staggered by the variety and quantity on offer. 'How do you get it?' I asked.

'Just choose what you want and download it, it's all free.' I realised that this world was infinite. It was like being let loose in a magazine store. If I could only get my own internet connection I could have all this stuff — and more. It was enthralling and I was immediately even more hooked. I wanted to open windows to machines on the other side of the world in the same way I did on my local machine. I wanted this internet and I wanted this graphical interface and I wanted it all now.

I took to my job easily. I was good at providing support, which was my main role. I talked to students and to staff. I learnt a lot about how the machines worked and stayed one step ahead of everyone else. I had some little power — I could order equipment, access all areas, borrow kit to take home. I expanded the Apple computer section for the creative side of the college and got to know more staff. I also started to learn just how corrupt the system was, not in a financial way, but in the way of controlling resources. On the other hand, I had some corrupt power of my own, I controlled some resources that other members of staff wanted. The job was frustrating, it seemed to move very slowly and I didn't get on very well with endless meetings. And I still couldn't get anyone to take my networking evangelism seriously.

I wasn't a traditional computer centre employee. I had no aptitude for nor interest in getting my fingers dirty with code and the 'real' staff laughed at me. I was a gentleman dilettante, good with people but rubbish with the inner secrets of machines, more interested in the stuff that was on the computers, what you could do with them and what was going to happen next. It was unusual, few arts and humanities graduates could do what I did, but at that time I wasn't considered useful as a support person. I came with little added value, but I knew that if I could find a way to get to this world I was made. It became my Narnia and from that point on I was constantly looking for the way through the back of a wardrobe into that strange world.

7

Finding Narnia

1992

Number of hosts breaks 1,000,000

Veronica, a gopherspace search tool, is released by Univ of Nevada

World Bank comes on-line

The term "surfing the Internet" is coined by Jean Armour Polly

Brendan Kehoe uses the term "net-surfing" as early as 6 June 1991 in a USENET post

Zen and the Art of the Internet is published by Brendan Kehoe (:jap:)

Internet Hunt started by Rick Gates

RFC 1300: Remembrances of Things Past

RFC 1313: Today's Programming for KRFC AM 1313 - Internet Talk Radio

Countries connecting to NSFNET: Antarctica (AQ), Cameroon (CM), Cyprus (CY), Ecuador (EC), Estonia (EE), Kuwait (KW), Latvia (LV), Luxembourg (LU), Malaysia (MY), Slovenia (SI), Thailand (TH), Venezuela (VE)

[HOBBES' INTERNET TIMELINE]

Out there, the Internet was coming. At Goldsmiths, even the local network didn't work. It was supposed to connect all the desktop PCs to the servers and to the printers. We had a lovely ex teacher who was responsible for networking internally, but he could never get it to work. He was having too much fun installing network cards and stroking his beard. His office was piled high with junk, each desktop a landslide of boxes, magazines, papers, kit, stuff. He spent days tinkering with each new card but didn't seem to understand why we were doing this.

The hippy got on well with the boss of the centre, another hippy academic with a full beard. He wrote notes on punch cards, showing his geeky authority. He was the first real geek I'd met and seemed to exist on a different planet and spent his time telling me tales of writing million-line programs in Cobalt.

We had a network officer, a clever woman who came from another part of London University. She knew a lot about networking, but she knew jack shit about the Internet. Nobody did, nobody wanted to know anything. They all thought that their chosen system which was invented in Europe and based in academia and large institutions, would be just perfect. I looked at what was happening with TCP/IP in America and I just knew a tsunami was coming.

The department bought all the equipment for a proper internet connection, which involved a radio link across the rooftops to Imperial College in town. But somehow it just didn't get installed, the boxes sat under her desk week after week. There was no faith, there was always something else needing more attention. After a meeting someone told me the honest truth. 'It will never happen, because it's Ivan's project'.

The whole internet could not arrive at this college because they didn't believe me. I wasn't happy.

That Christmas someone booked our meal at a restaurant in south London. Most of the staff were south London residents, and this suburb was natural territory. 'It's called Sophie's Choice,' they said. Was it named after the book, or the film, or was the owner called Sophie? I was gobsmacked. I talked to Wendy, I said I wasn't sure I could go. She laughed at my fears. 'Do you know what the book is about?' I said. 'It's alright' she replied, 'They don't all dress as Nazis or anything.' To my shame I went to the meal and enjoyed myself. Years later I was driving through south London when I saw the place again. It was real and it had no shame and it's still there to this day with nobody seeming to question the insanity of it all.

And then, in the middle of all this yearning, I discovered that there was an actual way into this world already set up and all I had to do was sign up. I did that and stepped through the back of a wardrobe into the actual Internet. Only it wasn't quite that simple.

I was in my office at Goldsmiths, reading a computer magazine, and I came across story about a company called Demon Internet that had won an award. Their product was an Internet access package called the Tenner a Month Internet. I knew that I had found what I was looking for. I had an account within a week.

I had missed the launch of Demon and only came across it by chance, sitting in my office at Goldsmiths. My world was totally disconnected, there was no social media, no Twitter to spread the word, no Facebook, not even mobile phones. The only people using online services were already online — and there weren't a lot of them as I'd found out already with my attempt at an artists' bulletin board.

The idea for the service had started in online chat room, CIX (Compulink Information eXchange), an online system that provided conference and chat features and built a committed community of UK users in a way that would look familiar to today's entrepreneurs. It had been running since 1883, initially using a FidoNet bulletin board. In 1987 it relaunched as a commercial service, offering access to some internet services such as Usenet. In time there was a discussion around 'real' internet access: how many customers would justify the cost of a leased line and were there enough interested parties in the UK to cover the bills? A member called Cliff Stanford decided to try it and see, and very quickly it turned from an experiment within the inner sanctum of online geekdom to a roaring commercial success. In addition to changing the world of internet access by chasing the price down as far as it could possibly go, Demon was also the first company to crowdsource their own startup.

Signing up for a Demon account turned out to be the easy bit. I had to set it up, but the account came with no software and no installation routine. It was almost as if it was designed to test your ability to work it all out for yourself: there was no manual. All I got was a London dial up number and a sheet of information about how to wangle a connection. I spent the next month trying to make it work, then trying to work out if it was working.

It was possibly the most painful learning curve of my life and I loved every minute of it.

I thought I knew something about computers, but I didn't tell anyone what I was doing because I didn't want to be exposed to ridicule. I was already the most computer literate person I knew apart from my colleagues. I spent my working week sitting in front of machines and teaching people about them, but now I was embarking on something new in the world and I felt vulnerable. I set about collecting the necessaries for going online.

The documentation that came with my Demon account suggested using something called KAQ9A to get online. KAQ9A was a primitive program, originally written for radio enthusiasts to transmit their radio signals over networks. It ran under DOS, which I was familiar with, but it was tricky to get running. I was at the height of my DOS skills but even so it was a huge struggle. Eventually, bang! I had the real internet in my own house.

It's hard to describe just what I had, though. It wouldn't be recognisable to today's users.

The world came into my house through the phone line into the basement, into my small PC and on to my Apple Mac, giving me a miniature Local Area Network, all plugged together with wires and bits of hardware.

In a time when we have always on Internet over Wi-Fi for our laptops, our phones and out tablets and can connect from the street, from our cars, from cafes and restaurants, it's hard to remember a time when we had none of that. Making a connection into my house to one computer took a few weeks and once I had it I was not going to let it go, ever.

The entire world was at my fingertips, sort of. I finally had the internet I had seen the year before. Although I had to dial up through a very cheap (and slow) modem and I had to make that connection each time I wanted to go online, I knew I was finally a master of the universe.

The Internet of 1992 was nothing like the online world we know today. There wasn't much there there. It was a crawling protean sort of place where many life forms flourished in primitive versions of what was to come. The Cambrian explosion was close but had not yet happened. Despite this it seemed a hugely exciting place, ripe with potential. I thought what was there was fascinating and I could see a lot more was coming. It seemed like a publisher's vision of heaven, only it wasn't quite there yet.

We are now as far from those days as 1992 was from the cultural rebellions of 1968, but we understand a lot less about them.

This internet, as I soon found out, was a strange place. It wasn't barren, it had all the necessities for some kind of life, but only primitive forms had come into being. It was like a planet that had cooled from the gaseous state and was waiting for life to evolve. There were interesting people around, but they were mainly technophiles or academic professionals.

Interestingly, there were lots of artists.

There had been artists from my first encounter with the primitive networks. It seemed that we were excited by the potential of this new space and were capable of understanding the potential for basic tools to generate work. From the first time I went online I found people who were exchanging art, in the manner of mail networks, sending images across the world, modifying them and passing them on again.

I started to mine the riches of the Internet and I looking for a project. I wasn't conscious of my search, it was just something that I did. I had a habit of institutionalising my interests and then converting them into publications.

The internet consisted of a lot of different tools to move around, to share information and to find stuff. The tools had names like Archie and Veronica and WAIS and FTP and email. Archie

Veronica

WAIS

Ftp

Email

The networks had been developing for quite a long time, but the web itself was just a few sites thrown up by early adopters. Although I was working in a computer centre, my life revolved around art. I had my own personal factory premises behind my house and was a founder of Loophole Cinema which I was loving. I was fascinated by the networks and tried to get things going there, but it was hard work.

When I mentioned the Internet to people they tended to laugh and tell me it was a fad. 'It's like CB radio,' they would say. Citizen's Band Radio, a DIY sort of communication system that existed outside the restraints of telecoms, had swept across the western world a few years before, creating an industry of hardware and software, magazines and millionaires, before disappearing almost overnight. People who said this were accurate in their assumptions about what the Internet was, but for the wrong reasons. They assumed that the Internet had no value and would not last whereas really it was another communication system that existed outside government control. And this one had legs.

Although I was working in a computer centre, I was no techie. I could not code. I didn't really understand how computers worked. I was good at understanding how to make things happen and superb at explaining to other uncomprehending students how to get the computers to do what they wanted, but beyond that I had no real technology skills. I had become fairly adept at DOS, the primeval operating system that almost all the computers ran on at the time, and could explain the intricacies of Wordperfect, the writing tool that dominated life back then. There were no mice, no Windows type interfaces, no network, no internet, nothing. Just a bunch of standalone computers sitting in an old science lab.

I made an abstract piece of work using this coding language called HTML which, unlike other coding languages, seemed pretty easy to work out and use. It was hosted on the Goldsmiths computers. I had made the first html artwork.

I had realised that what was being called 'surfing' was more like what the Situationists called 'derive' or drift. I was a believer. I knew what was coming — I just didn't know how we were going to get there.

I struggled during those years to get anyone to listen to what I was trying to tell them: I knew the networks were coming but nobody was interested. In Switzerland, Tim Berners-Lee was suffering his own kickbacks. In 1991 he had presented his hypertext project to management in the hope that they would green-light expansion, but nothing happened. Those in his community who came across his project were enthusiastic but getting the resources to spread it outside that community was difficult.

In the academic world, things moved slowly. Europe was in thrall to an international system called OSI. It was a centralised set of protocols, paid for by the EU and researched by various universities around Europe. The project was slow and laborious. It was supposed to be technically excellent, but to me it just looked like a horror story in waiting. In the UK we used a set of books to define the parts of the system. Each book had a different coloured cover and was known by that colour. The set was called the Rainbow Book. It was like a hippies dream and I hadn't forgotten, never trust a hippy.

Across the pond a thing called the internet was using TCP/IP. When this came up at Goldsmiths it was rejected in scathing terms. Having learned my outsider lessons well with punk, I thought it sounded like a good idea. I had no idea what it meant technically, but for practical purposes I liked what I was hearing. That a lot of software was being written for this system, that it was moving fast and was taking over networking. I started to agitate for a proper internet connection. I wanted to continue with the mission.

At the beginning of the nineties, the UK was still using an ancient version of the addressing system. We had our domain name system back to front. There were many and varied reasons for this, most of them could be trotted off by a technician at will. It meant that my address at Goldsmiths was i.pope@uk.ac.gold. The .uk was at the wrong end. It was symptomatic of what was wrong with computing in Britain. There probably was nothing wrong with it in an historic sense. But I felt change. The time had come for a new order.

Suddenly a real internet book appeared and validated everything I was thinking. It made me realise I had to make a move. in 1989 Ed Krol had written a famous document, The Hitchhiker's Guide To The Internet. The title was a reference to Douglas Adams' Hitchhiker's Guide to the Galaxy, which was itself a titular descendant of a 1971 book, The Hitch-hiker's Guide to Europe. That book had inspired me to set off around Europe at the end of the seventies. My journey was coming full circle.

Krol's guide to the Internet carried the admonition, '*In cases of major discrepancy it is always reality that's got it wrong. And remember, DON'T PANIC*'. In 1991 he expanded the document into a whole book with the same attitude and called it The Whole Internet User's Guide and Catalogue. It was the first book that was not only about the internet but was structured like the internet. In other words, it wasn't about the technical operation of the networks but about what one could find on them, what they could be used for.

It changed everything.

I decided that I had to tell the world about this thing I had found, and fast. I became an evangelist. I carried the internet meme and I was now contagious and I knew what the transmission route was: a magazine. I went back to my roots and started planning a publication, to be called The World Wide Web Newsletter .

8

Only Connect

Internet Timeline 1993

InterNIC created by NSF to provide specific Internet services:

directory and database services (AT&T)

registration services (Network Solutions Inc.)

information services (General Atomics/CERFnet)

US White House email comes on-line at whitehouse.gov; web site launches in 1994

President Bill Clinton: president whitehouse.gov

Vice-President Al Gore: vice-president whitehouse.gov

Worms of a new kind find their way around the Net - WWW Worms

(W4), joined by Spiders, Wanderers, Crawlers, and Snakes ...

Internet Talk Radio begins broadcasting (:sk2:)

United Nations (UN) comes on-line (:vgc:)

US National Information Infrastructure Act

Businesses and media begin taking notice of the Internet

.sk (Slovakia) and .cz (Czech Republic) created after split of Czechoslovakia; .cs decommissioned

InterCon International KK (IIKK) provides Japan's first commercial Internet connection in September. TWICS, though an IIKK leased line, begins offering dial-up accounts the following month (:tb1:)

Mosaic takes the Internet by storm (22 Apr); WWW proliferates at a 341,634% annual growth rate of service traffic. Gopher's growth is 997%.

RFC 1437: The Extension of MIME Content-Types to a New Medium

RFC 1438: IETF Statements of Boredom (SOBs)

Countries connecting to NSFNET: Bulgaria (BG), Costa Rica

(CR), Egypt (EG), Fiji (FJ), Ghana (GH), Guam (GU), Indonesia

(ID), Kazakhstan (KZ), Kenya (KE), Liechtenstein (LI), Peru

(PE), Romania (RO), Russian Federation (RU), Turkey (TR),

Ukraine (UA), UAE (AE), US Virgin Islands (VI)

[Hobbes' Internet Timeline]

At the beginning of 1993, despite my optimism for this new world, nobody had a computer and nobody understood or wanted email, let alone any other online services. It wasn't that they couldn't have done with them, they could, it was a total conceptual void. The problem was, nobody knew what I was talking about.

My short lived ArtNet experiment had taught me that. Except for a few pioneers in the small online communities, the idea that you could have friends that you talked to every day but never met would have seemed preposterous, but I had already started down that road. I was probing the online community of artists who, as always, had formed an experimental vanguard, eager to explore this new territory. My love affair with online was still rooted firmly in the arts world.

It was a complex, busy time in which my art and my internet ran in precise parallel until something had to give. The sun shone through that year and I was free. I knew I was going to publish my magazine, which gave me gnawing anxiety but was now unstoppable. I pushed these two projects in parallel for the first part of the year, but eventually I decided to leave my job. I'd had enough of the constraints of a university computer centre with no interest in the internet.

We didn't realise it at the time, but the beach we were now standing on had formed because all the water had suddenly rushed out, like at the seafront before a tsunami. We were like the innocent holidaymakers who, seeing the shoreline recede unexpectedly, were idly wandering further and further out, picking up exotic fish and strange seaplants and never, not once, looking up to notice the vast unimaginable wave that was gathering in the offing and which was going to sweep back in and wash us all to our doom. We had no idea what we were playing on.

All I knew was that I had suddenly found a beach and I was determined to enjoy it. The internet was there, beneath the pavement, it was just that nobody had thought to pull up the cobblestones to find it.

It had been developing beneath our feet for over thirty years. It was a military-academic project to be sure, but the basic parts had been in place for a long time. The networks that it rode upon came and went. The first node in the network outside the US was in London, at UCL. It was installed in 19xx. But an internet built for and by academics, with help from the American military-industrial industry, with development by the post-libertarian sandal shod hippy academics on the West Coast, the same seedbed that would generate Silicon Valley and the explosive growth of technology and social media twenty-five years later.

But for the moment, these networks were a secret hidden in plain sight. Academics and researchers used them and extended them and created tools for themselves, but nobody wanted to tell the general public about it. Of course, there was little use the public at large would have for a packet switching network. The public didn't even have computers. This was the situation I ran up against in my evangelical fervour after I stumbled across this new world. Then, in a moment of exquisite beauty, a British man working in Switzerland at an international physics research project came up with an elegant new tool for information management. He called it the World Wide Web and new epoch was born.

We entered a strange interregnum where the online world was struggling to be born while a short lived industry was growing up to take the word to the offline world. There were good reasons for this. There was money to be made in the established publishing world and a new subject that was getting attention and generating excitement seemed like a surefire hit, while nobody had the slightest clue of how to earn money online. Although there were people throwing commercial internet ideas around, they were at a very early stage and there was much cynicism as to whether it would ever be possible. Most of the commentary about the internet was being done by academics and librarians. In the US, a librarian, Jean Armour Polly, wrote a guide to the internet at the end of 1992 and, coining a phrase, called it *Surfing the INTERNET*. There was some pre internet publishing that fascinated me. I was also reading a Newsletter called Inside Multimedia which was produced by a cha y guy called John Barker. The mag listed him as Editor, Publisher and Typesetter — an approach that grated somewhat but gave me a model of what I wanted to do. I could assemble a similar Newsletter about the internet on my own and scoop the market.

Around this time I started to change, the internet started to actually change who I was, how I thought. We now understand more how the internet changes people, how connectivity fundamentally alters your relationship to the world, how the reward system of social media hooks and addicts users very quickly. The process must have applied itself to me along the way because somewhere in the months after my acquisition of a full internet connection I started to become a different person.

It can't have happened very quickly because, for one thing, there weren't that many people online and there wasn't much to do. There wasn't much online that could fundamentally change one. It was really the fact of connection that started the process. I was becoming modern, I was entering the new world. It was going to take a few years, possibly two decades, but I was on my way.

I was different to the person I had been when I'd arrived in London, different to the art student who had arrived at Goldsmiths. I had outgrown my view that I had done most things, that as I was older than most of those around me I didn't really have much to prove. I had entered a more adult environment. More to the point, I was inventing a space to work and play in, one that didn't yet exist. I knew instinctively how to create that world but at the same time I had no concept of how to manage it once I had created it. I was as isolated and singular as I had ever been. All the electronic networks in the world couldn't really get me over my fundamental lack of self belief. At the same time, my ability to grasp bigger pictures, to understand the landscape I was looking at, came into play and I launched myself into the jet stream of culture. The attention deficit was kicking in and this time it worked well for me. I had the big picture vision, the epiphany and the ability to dump what wasn't working, what seemed a dead end. Although I didn't know it, my disorder was driving me forward.

The rest of the world would have to follow me, for better or for worse, into the abyss.

I wanted to evangelise this amazing thing that I had found, that was just getting better and better each day. It was fine talking about it online, the drawback was that everyone on the internet was already a convert. Everyone online knew about online but there were no channels to evangelise people who were offline. I needed to find a way to shout about it, to tell the world what was happening. I thought I should make a magazine about the internet.

Once this idea had occurred to me I was unstoppable. Because I was familiar with industry Newsletter s I thought I could create a niche publication, to inform and update the business world about what was happening on the internet. I decided to launch a Newsletter . I worked myself up into a state of excitement, imagining that I would earn a living selling subscriptions to a trade Newsletter .

To get going, I started to collect everything I could find on the subject. Using Quark DTP, on the fancy new Apple Mac systems, I started work on the design, layout, writing and editing of my first issue.

A first I thought I was entirely on my own, but I soon realised there were others out there in the darkness. In quick succession I came across two Newsletter s, first The Internet Business Review and then The Internet Business Journal. Both were edited by a man called Christopher Locke. Locke was a driving force in the embryonic commercial internet realm, moving swiftly from project to project and providing inspirations along the way.

Locke burned a whirlwind path through the early internet landscape. He also turned up as head of the short lived Meckler-Web a year later. This was supposed to be an all singing all dancing centralised web publishing project but Alan Meckler canned it as it was being launched.

"On Friday October 14, 1994 Alan Meckler remade Meckler-Web into the very hardcopy publishing, advertising-based structure that Chris Locke, its creator had said could never work in the new electronic world of the Internet. Indeed MecklerWeb will now be run on the very attributes of print publishing that Locke set out to prove no longer viable when he created it."

Locke went off to MCA and then IBM and later became RageBoy, helping to launch The Cluetrain Manifesto, the internet's answer to Martin Luther and his ninety-six theses. Cluetrain was a punk manifesto for the internet, a ranting take no prisoners understanding that passed most people by.

The commercial exploitation of the internet as a subject had barely started but the mad founders were gathering speed.

In April 1993 Alan Meckler, an American publisher with interests in the world of librarians and information science, had launched what must be the first internet magazine: Internet World. The first issue was a monochrome sixteen page Newsletter edited by Daniel P. Dern, a technology writer who had graduated from MIT.

For some reason, half the publication covered developments in Britain including a list of ten 'UK internet connections'. It also contained a review of a book called The Smiley Dictionary: Cool Things to Do with Your Keyboard, written by an early incarnation of Seth Godin who later became a publishing phenomenon. All in all it was a strangely turgid affair, reflecting its roots in library science (formally it was a continuation of a publication called Research & Education Networking). Dern's editorial promoted an upcoming conference to be called Information Network, which seems to have never happened. It almost certainly morphed along the way into the first UK Internet World event, which took place in 1994 and was subtitled Document Delivery World International. The domains of library and computer were merging, on their way to becoming an entirely new world.

Dern hadn't grasped the essential excitement of the internet at that point but within a year of launch the magazine became a full colour newsstand publication with a paid circulation of 50,000 copies.

As life got more complicated, Loophole Cinema became more successful. Word of our ability to create stunning site specific installations spread and we started to get invited to take part in bigger events. We expanded and things became more complicated: more people meant more voices, more ideas and more arguments. We had already sucked a couple of friends from my Goldsmiths days into the crew, Bea Haut and Ruth Lander. Greg also recruited a friend, artist and filmmaker, Paul Rogers who worked at Central St Martins art school. There was no method of making decisions and no hierarchy, except that, as always, the filmmakers seemed to be in charge of everything. We still used Temple Works as a base to create and test equipment and to shoot film and take photos, but the sites for our events exploded out into the industrial world.

The Filmmakers' Co-op remained a key part of the equation and Greg and Paul continued to make films for our events there, using processes that I never got to grips with. I was interested in film and the opportunities the co-op offered, but I was increasingly busy with my own developments in the online world.

We decided we had to have someone in the group to develop and generate sounds and we advertised in various places for someone, anyone. We didn't really know what we wanted but assumed we'd know it when we found it. After pondering an application from a percussionist who has been working on Nico's most recent album, we eventually alighted on a New Zealander, Ben Hayman, who was a programmer at a bank with a studio near Old Street. He was handy with technical equipment, he spoke our language and, most importantly, we got on well with him. Ben joined Loophole. That is to say, he became a part of us by a sort of form of osmosis. Loophole still barely existed outside any particular project we had on. Through Lois Keidan, who had left the Arts Council and set up her own performance organisation, we were invited to take part in an event at the ICA, Shot in the Dark, for April. This event took place in the ICA theatre and the budget for the show allowed us to get a huge curtain made up professionally onto which to project our shadows. Goldsmiths had acquired (at my urging) an LCD panel that fitted over an overhead projector. For the first time I could integrate video imagery into a show. Video projectors at this time were huge three lens items that tended to be fixed into place - the time of cheap small projectors had not yet arrived. For imagery I used a biology videodisk which I connected to the little Apple Mac from college. I wrote a Hypercard program to control the selection of random imagery, the only time I successfully wrote my own software, such as it was. Videodisks were already semi-obsolete technology, but I always liked that sort of product best and it meant that nobody really argued with me borrowing everything. The show at the ICA wasn't the best example of Loophole work. We never really flourished in institutional spaces and the theatre setting was just too constrained for our anarchy, but at least it brought us to notice and gave us some credibility. Also, although I didn't know it at the time, I had just done my first event in that theatre. My next would be something special and entirely internet based.

In June we got involved in a night of performance and partying at the then derelict and squatted Brockwell Lido in South London. The lido had been closed down a few years before and left to rot before being occupied by the usual suspects from London's alternative community. We went along to have a look and ended up spending a week building a show out of things we found on the site alongside the empty swimming pool. The event was preceded by a heatwave and we spent days in blasting sunshine constructing our madness, pushing the Loophole aesthetic forward.

Fire, film, wind and shadow projection cabinets built in 9 metal changing room lockers spanning a corner of the empty outdoor swimming pool. Live performance involving the operation and investigation of these cabinets including miniature shadow theatres, light manipulation, distress flares and constructed sound scape.

On the night the huge space filled up very quickly, leaving excited crowds outside in the hot summer night. All around the site performers circulated with the crowd and projections and performances were everywhere. Outside a crowd gathered, locked out from the sold out space. I found a line of people climbing over a laddder at the back wall and went to help my friend Richard from Temple Works over. He handed me a small wrap of amphetamine sulphate and my evening took off with a rush.

We had filled a line of metal lockers with dried plants we gathered from around the site. When the time came we lit them. We had carefully converted them into chimneys by cutting air passages top and bottom, and they went up with a whoosh, illuminating the night and almost setting the crowd, which was pressing in to our space, alight. I lit a flare and ran around the cabinets, holding it high in the air, illuminating the close faces of the crowd with an unreal red glow. The projectors fired up and Bea reflected their imagery with a sheet of polished steel.

It was over quickly but some magic had been achieved that night. We'd conquered fire and made the most dramatic show of the night and we were in control of our world, performers with a watching crowd and it felt good.

The next month we were given an even more bigger and more dramatic opportunity. A group from Birmingham, the Fine Rats (a play on Fine Arts, I always thought it a bit cheap, a bit stupid), were putting on a show in an empty tower block on a hill on the edge of the city. Two twenty storey blocks had been emptied in preparation for demolition. They were sealed and had no power or water, but we decided to repeat our process of living in for a week beforehand. We took a small petrol generator with us and were given access to the forbidding edifice — a grey looming structure swaddled at the base with steel barriers to prevent any entry. The ground floors were grim and dark but as we climbed higher into the building it became a light and airy space, albeit an abandoned and dirty one. Each floor contained six flats and every flat showed evidence of previous occupants from elegant tidy wallpapered spaces to trashed graffitied rooms. The building had been a decanting space for difficult tenants at the end of its life, a sink estate, gaining a reputation as a dangerous place, although now it just looked sad, containing only the merest detritus of the thousands who had passed through. I liked that you could walk into any flat and get a different vibe, imagine someone once lavishing love on this place in the sky, on safety, on warmth and security. That had gone long before we arrived and we were about to further demolish any traces of it. We took up residence on the eleventh floor and placed our generator on the balcony so as not to kill ourselves..

For our show we chose the sixth floor, taking the whole space for a Loophole installation unlike anything we'd done before. We slowly built a sequence of projections between all the flats and down the corridors. We took sledgehammers and punched holes through walls to reveal tableaux that we built in sealed rooms. For the first time we had complete freedom to make any damage we liked in the pursuit of our vision, and we didn't hold back. By the time we had finished the floor was riddled with cabling and holes, we had made a nightmare dreamscape with film loops running the length of the passages and four of the flats joined by a maze of punctures. We kept the final two flats for a live performance on the night.

My friend Richard, from the tiny house next to Temple Works went off to do a degree at Newport College of Art. After starting he phoned me up.

'They need a new lecturer here, the guy has just left, you should apply.'

I'd never heard of the college, but it sounded interesting. The artist who had just left was Paul Sermon, who was going to create waves in the interactive art world, and the course itself was run by a legendary figure from computers and art, Roy Asco .

Roy had been making work and theorising about it since the sixties and had been involved in various legendary events in the field. He was then Professor of Technoetic Arts at the University of Wales. He invited me down for a visit and then gave me a teaching post, very part time, in his department which was based outside Newport at the Roman town of Caerleon. I cannot remember whether I was teaching telematics in the department of Telemedia or Telemedia in the department of Telematics, but I had found someone who thinking and working in the space I was keen to expand on. Asco had been doing this since the sixties — the nascent area of art and networking had a longer history then I'd ever imagined and I'd just met its guru. I had found a trump card which was also a weakness. I knew enough about the internet to teach and was fired up enough to teach it, but the college had no connection to the networks. I made a series of rash promises and when I started work they grandly gave me a telephone extension and an old Apple Mac. I took my own modem and attempted to connect to the world, but it was hard going. Roy was supportive but distant, the students, sensing he was on his own planet, called him the Spaceman. And, although I was broke and the money from Newport was useful, it was very hard to travel up and down and stay in town for a day and a half each week. Richard came to the rescue, putting me up in his squalid student house where I slept on a redundant bed in a spare room full of junk and tried to avoid ever eating anything prepared in the revolting kitchen.

I felt I was in a holding pa ern, but there were more interesting things in my life then ever before — and I had a small income again.

To get my internet magazine started, I worked on it during working hours in my job. It started as a Newsletter , but grew and grew until it was a magazine. When it was done it was ugly and thin, but it was an Internet magazine and it had an electrifying effect on the people who came across it. It was the first Web magazine in the world.

At the end of April, as the magazine came to fruition, I left my job, the only job I'd ever had, and pulled my tiny pension out to fund the launch. I'd been there for two years, that seemed long enough. I then had to fall back on my own resources, which included an internet connection and my computers and printers, including the tiny Apple Mac. I took it home with me. I had enough on hand to pay for the first couple of issues. In financial terms, and in writing and producing it, the thing would became overwhelming, but in the first flush, in producing the first issue, I was in heaven and didn't care what happened next.

It was the same pa ern, the attention deficit that had formed the pa ern of my life since I was young. It gave me an ability to see, to really see what was in the world, and to pluck insights from the air. Better, my combination of attributes more or less mandated me to turn my ideas into businesses. No, not really businesses. Later I came to understand what I was doing and I started calling the process *institutionalising*. My habit was to look for a structure, for an institution to contain what is bugging me. These structures could take different forms, and had been doing so since I was a child, writing plans for school organisations in my bed at night. What is true is that it wasn't that I lusted to be a businessman, an entrepreneur. It didn't really matter what form I ended up with, the desire was to try and rustle something up. I was entrepreneurial, in that I was always willing to take the chance, to make the leap and to tell people what I was doing as if it was real. That was part of the magic. Inside I didn't feel very confident. I knew I was doing something right but I thought I could also see how ridiculous my efforts were.

Almost everyone I met thought I was mad. A genius, perhaps, but mad. Magnificently, spectacularly mad, but mad all the same. I had left a secure job to start a daft magazine on a subject of interest to almost no-one. For a few months, this seemed true. Then the world exploded. The World Wide Web Newsletter was the first Internet magazine with any sort of a consumer orientation, that looked at the Internet and the emerging Web from a nontechnical perspective. It only lasted four issues, but at the start it seemed like a natural and logical process. I'd grown up in a newspaper environment, making publications was deep in my psyche and I still believed in the attitude from the punk years: just get up and do it.

So I did.

I had no idea how many people, if anyone, would subscribe to it. I didn't even know how many people were interested in the Internet by then, but I knew, somewhere deep inside myself, that a huge thing was rumbling towards me. I thought, you've got one chance. I knew it was now or never, that others would follow close behind. I didn't articulate these thoughts though. I didn't even tell anyone else what I was doing. I just started obsessing on putting a publication together, as if it would be easy.

I knew that I was participating in a large scale project and that if I hit the ground running I could position myself at the centre of it. I was so separated from my natural milieu that when I chose the name The World Wide Web Newsletter it didn't occur to me to try and make contact with Tim Bernard-Lee, to check that he was alright with my blatant theft of his name. I just thought that the Web was the most interesting thing happening on the Internet at that point and I wanted to be associated with it.

I looked at my world as a candy box from which I could assemble what I needed. This was the double edge curse of my attention deficit: it made me a genius for ideas and at the same time made me unable to integrate in any world. I was a loner, that was sure, but now I was a loner on a mission. So long as there was momentum, I was safe. Only when I lost attention was I lost.

I didn't have much idea how to assemble a magazine and the thought of finding a designer never crossed my mind. I suppose I was as much in love with the technology as the product. I put the editorial in the wrong place and left an early date on it so that a magazine that came out at the end of August 1993 had an editorial dated for July. None of that seemed to matter. I finally had my magazine and it was a real first, and it came out of my tiny basement in Hackney. I found a great image for the cover from NASA, an Apollo rocket taking off. I didn't think through the metaphor I was using, but it worked. Inside I had found some contributors. Neville Wilford reviewed a new brower, Cello, and I persuaded a real internet celebrity, John S. Makulowich, to write a column, Awesome Sites. I wrote a long piece about email. I wrote about the UK networks and listed nineteen internet access providers, although only three of them provided full IP access. I was determined to make the industry exist. I had one page on the World Wide Web including the Vatican Library and an experimental map browser being run by Xerox Research Center in Palo Alto. I wrote about Buddhists Online, a page about becoming an astronaut. I reviwed Ed Krol's book, The Whole Internet User's Guide and Catalog, and admi ed it's part in my magazine, '*I'll admit here that this publication was inspired in part by this book.*'

Almost everything I wrote about would not be recognisable to anyone online today. In the (Re)Source section at the back I explained how you could use email to retrieve files from FTP sites and how you could Telnet to World Wide Web sites. The system was a kludge, but it was a glorious kludge. On the back page I gave my List of Lists, a key to a part of the limitless resources that were now out there.

It was heroic and my world exploded into life. The World Wide Web Newsletter was the first Internet magazine with any sort. I was on an evangelistic roll, swept up in a fervour of belief. Looking back now it is easy to take it all for granted but at the time I was speaking from my heart and I was crying in the wilderness.

9

The World Wide Web
Newsletter

Only connect! ... Live in fragments no longer.

Welcome to Cyberspace. This magazine is about a reality, about something that you can take part in and use now. It may seem like science fiction, but it exists. This is Desktop Global Networking. The global networks are without definition. They are composed of myriad users, the millions of us who cruise the highways, netsurfing on a sea of data.

Thirty-three years ago, Ted Nelson posited a concept of Hypertext in which all the information in the world would be linked through electronic bridges. Today that dream starts to look like reality. You can link up, and it won't cost you a huge fortune. You can join in, and there are real world resources and uses out there. It's not just for computer nuts – it is ordinary people using the nets that makes them real. A critical mass has been passed. The tools we are now seeing make yesterdays text terminals seem light-years away, but millions of us still rely on them, and millions more have no access at all – yet.

This World Wide Web, this hyperspace, this cybernet, demands constant attention. It is the mission of the World Wide Web Newsletter to pay that attention, to keep tabs on the fast changing inter and outer net that comprises this new continent.

This Newsletter is aimed as much at those on the outside looking in as those on the inside looking, well, looking.

The World Wide Web Newsletter aims to link those on the outside to those on the inside, to link developments in the commercial realm to those elsewhere, to bring news and developments and to encourage use and exploration of this new continent.

The Internet is in flux – we have no idea what tools and resources next year will bring, let alone the next five or ten. This is indeed a new continent, and I hope you will come along to explore.

I had an instinctive feeling that this is what the internet was for - living in fragments no longer — but I had to work out what came after the fragments. The pressing question was what to put in the magazine. Although it was named after the World Wide Web, it was a magazine about the internet. The Web was so new that there was very little to write about, I certainly didn't see it taking over the world. At the time there were lots of different parts of the internet and they were all fascinating and I was determined to track them all. Amongst the mass of information and data online I started looking for actual news stories, things that would work from a magazine perspective. I thought a lot about sections, what areas the mag should cover.

More browsers were starting to appear, all of them internal project at universities. In March that year, the University of Kansas released the Lynx 2.0 browser, based on a non-internet hypertext browser they had already developed. At the National Center for Supercomputing Applications (NCSA) at the University of Illinois a small team, including student Marc Andreessen, created the Mosaic browser.

As Tim Berners-Lee later pointed out, Andreessen had a different approach to the Web and the browser.

'Marc maintained a near-constant presence on the news groups discussing the Web, listening for features people were asking for, what would make browsers easier to use. He would program these into the nascent browser and keep publishing new releases so others could try it. He listened intently to critiques, almost as if he were a ending to 'consumer relations'. Marc was not so much interested in just making the program work as in having his browser used by as many people as possible. That was, of course, just what the Web needed.'

Mosaic was much more of a product than other browsers and it was easy to use. This was the sort of thing I was looking for, what interested me. I wasn't a programmer, I couldn't work out how to use browsers that ran under Unix or needed arcane environments. I wanted stuff that just did what I knew the internet was good for — allowed an environment for publishing of one sort or another. The Mosaic browser was so successful so quickly that for a short period the world started referring to the entire internet as 'Mosaic'. Even Berners-Lee noticed this.

'The media ... started to portray Mosaic as if it were equivalent to the Web.'

One of the many other tools that made up the internet at that time was called Gopher. It was a graphical interface to information but it related to folders and documents rather than the content of documents. It rapidly became popular and the University of Minnesota, who owned it, thought they had spotted a revenue opportunity. They announced that there would be a licence fee for some classes of users, mainly commercial companies. This was like a rocket to the adoption of Gopher, as the existence of a licence immediately made developing for and expanding on the protocol a very dangerous choice. There was always the potential for the University to claim intellectual property rights over someone else's work. Even if this was unlikely, the chances of lawyers sanctioning investment and commercial development on the platform was killed off overnight. Berners-Lee recognised the danger that this route posed to his own nascent product and others started to ask him about it. He returned to CERN and pushed to have the protocol and code placed in the public domain. On April the 30th this was done.

On April 7th, Berners-Lee sent out an email to www mailing lists announcing World Wide Web Software Put Into Public Domain. I carefully printed out and saved his announcement.

> *With the Web, we are sharing knowledge without discrimination as to who or where in the world you are. The W3 developers look forward to a time when the Internet, and so the Web, will be accessible from homes and high schools anywhere. As well as an opening up of research ideas and educational material for all tastes and ages.*

Although the announcement passed almost all of the world by, it was monumental in changing the world. If Berners-Lee hadn't persuaded CERN to put his invention into the public domain so that anyone could use it without any restrictions, it may never have become as successful as it did. Software that carries any form of restriction or ownership, even if the owners assert they aren't going to do anything with it, makes lawyers very nervous and companies stay away. With the World Wide Web, the April 7 announcement changed the entire game. For me, it should be World Internet Day.

As the first issue of my magazine neared completion, my other project, Loophole Cinema, were offered as slot at the prestigious European Media Arts Festival in Germany. It would be my last major work with them.

We knew we had to go, although it would be our most complicated gig so far. Transport was always our big problem as our assortment of dodgy old cars wouldn't get us and our equipment all the way to Germany. We knew it was going to be just the perfect gig, bigger than anything we had done before, and we started work on planning immediately. We hadn't been overseas as a group before, it was complicated enough carrying our ever-accumulating piles of junk, projectors and machines around the country. Now we had a real challenge.

Setting off in the mini convoy for Germany, I left instructions for the delivery of my first print run. My brother said he'd visit us and bring some copies with him.

The festival organiser had indeed done us proud: giving us the remains of a vast German steelworks called Klockner Werk that had been closed down and was partially demolished. The site sat on the edge of Osnabruck. As we settled down to a week of hard work, rigging vast screens and sounds systems in the remaining sheds, the locals soon noticed our presence. At the weekend they came in their cars and drove slowly around the site, gazing at us. We had three interconnected sheds to build our biggest work to date in. The sheds were so huge that in the night we opened up the rolling shutter doors and drove our vehicles inside.

My brother had told me when he was arriving, but in the days before mobile phones meeting arrangements were a haphazard business. I took the group bicycle and rode to the station at the appointed time, but he wasn't on the train. We took our caravan into the sheds later that night and shut the doors down behind us, not knowing that he had turned up on a later train. He took a taxi to our site but found our doors firmly closed and no response. It must have been frightening, alone in the huge, deserted steelworks. After a while he returned to the station, to find it filled with the local junkies who took up night residence. In the early hours of the morning, completely frustrated, he returned to our site and lay down outside the doors.

It was only when we woke up and someone pressed the button to open the huge doors that we discovered a dishevelled, sleep deprived and thoroughly pissed off brother outside our den. He had the copies of my magazine that he had faithfully held on to all night, so while he went off to crash out in our wagon I got my first look at hard copies of the publication that I had created on screen.

I stood amid the ruins of the German economic miracle, in a factory which had been part of a Nazi war machine, holding the first evidence that a new revolution was in progress. I'd first taken the networks seriously during the final years of the Eastern bloc, when citizens had called out to the West using primitive communication systems. Now the internet was poised to enter our lives. At that time I had no idea how huge the coming changes were, but I'd done my bit. I was an evangelist and I now had a publication to prove it.

Our shows went well in our usual disorganised and chaotic manner. We drank too much and put on two sold out frenetic shows in the vast spaces. We basked in the sunshine and enjoyed ourselves before driving home again in mini convoy. My internet life was becoming real and my time with Loophole was coming to an end. I knew I'd created something that wasn't going to be so easy to abandon.

When we got home I had many boxes of my magazine to get out and sell. This was outside my comfort zone, I wasn't a good knocker on doors. I wrote a press release, made an email address of www@ukartnet.demon.co.uk and sent it out. Then I went around London, visiting computer shops, bookshops and art galleries, asking them if they would stock my magazine. The reaction was overwhelmingly good, everyone I asked was interested. Soon I was on sale in a variety of outlets from science fiction shops to the ICA bookshop on the Mall. I also found a distributor who took the magazine on and sent it around the country. It never sold a huge number of copies, but it seemed to get to a lot of the people who needed to see it and brought me a lot of feedback and attention. I soon discovered that there were people out there who were interested in the same thing as me.

We were reaching out for each other and were about to change the world.

The World Wide Web Newsletter brings you Desktop Global Networking

Now you can plug in to an endless world of people and resources for everyone. Al Gore dubbed it the 'information superhighway', now everyone from the President of the United States to the grungiest cyberpunk is out there, roaming the highways. The WORLD WIDE WEB

NEWSLETTER is a unique source of news, information, help, addresses and ideas from and about the new global networks. If you want to know about the cyberspace you need to read the World Wide Web Newsletter.

The WORLD WIDE WEB NEWSLETTER is proud to introduce Desktop Global Networking (DGN) for all. Anyone who has an interest in communication; anyone who is thinking about utilising the power of desktop global networking; anyone who should know what is happening out there; anyone interested in the range of resources and products that make up the World Wide Web has to read The World Wide Web Newsletter.

The September/October issue of The WORLD WIDE WEB NEWSLETTER:

+ UK Networking: how to; where to; what to — and a full listing of UK Internet access providers.

+ Powermail. The wonderful world of mailing lists: how to exploit the power of e-mail.

+ Cello. Full featured Internet software for Windows reviewed by Neville Wilford

+ Awesome Sites: Virtual Tourism, the John S. Makulowich column

+ NetNews. Latest news from the global networks

+ Off Internet. Hardware and software developments outside and around the Internet

+ Internet A-Z: Astronautics. How to become an astronaut and other frequently asked questions + Plus information on software and hardware developments, resource lists; publications; Internet

Multimedia and much more

If you don't read The WORLD WIDE WEB NEWSLETTER you'll never know what you are missing - or who's missing you.

There was now an embryonic commercial angle to the online world. Unlike a few years before, the notion of having pay for access to that world was no longer the interest of a tiny minority, and businesses were starting to pay attention. A range of tools were developed along with graphical interfaces and simpler to use tools which was making it easier to actually get online. The process of setting up a connection was still cumbersome and the benefits considered dubious by most. Anyone using the networks at this time will still have the singsong tune of the modem connection embedded in their memory. The frustration when that connection failed to work and the difficulty of using a home's only phone line for Internet use were off putting. Above all, the pain of a phone bill where every connection had to be paid for by the minute was frightening, especially as many people still had to dial long distance to connect.

Most people who did get online in this time would limit their online time as much as possible, getting on and off quickly before the bills mounted up, before someone else in the house screamed for the line to be released. All this, which to me seemed like the beginning of a new age, was also the last gasp of an old one. The networks were gaining acquiring the heft necessary to move mountains, and some very large mountains indeed were about to be shifted.

That same year the project that led to domain name registration at InterNIC was launched and a tiny company called Network Solutions was selected to run it. This tiny consultancy, based in Washington DC, was a minority owned company and thus qualified to be given a government contract worth a few million dollars. They built out a registration system for .com, .net and .org domain names, which were still a strange and unrecognised medium. I didn't know then what they were or what they did, but within a few years they would become the centre of my life.

Through friends at Cityscape in London, I registered my first domain name, 3W.com.

At this time, I still didn't really understand that I was surrounded by the seeds of a new generation, the millions of people whose lives were about to be changed by the internet. I didn't think of the work I was doing as anything to do with new opportunities, not even for myself. I thought of it as a project, almost a piece of art, which for technical reasons had to exist as a commercial project. In this way I was different to many of that early generation of believers. Most of my friends, when the networking bug struck them, took to creating projects that had no basis in commercial sense. My approach, on the other hand, was to try and set up something that earned real money, that was grounded in business. I had no real idea how to do this but it came from somewhere deep inside me, a drive to make revenue not just as a way to earn a living but as a way to validate my endeavours.

Not that I was any good at it. I had an almost pathological aversion to paperwork, to putting things in order. What it really boiled down to, I eventually came to realise, was an inability to keep returning to the same subject, a disorder of attention. I would let paperwork pile up endlessly until it was unapproachable, until the idea of dealing with it was unbearable. Then I would find a way to let it all go, to move on and find something new that satisfied me.

I also had no ability to write a plan, to make a budget, to finish an outline. I understood what these things were but again, something deep inside me didn't let me relate to them in a sensible fashion. I had no budget for my magazine, I had no plan, I winged it on a daily basis, allowing my belief and the drama of the moment to carry me forward, and of course after a while I found I had run out of money. Although I was uniquely in the right place at the right time again, I was woefully undercapitalised and, for some reason, I had no inclination to find anyone to discuss this with. I stayed in my own bubble. If anything, the separateness of the online world, where connection was made at one remove, suited me perfectly and allowed me to hide my behaviour even from myself.

When issue two of the World Wide Web Newsletter came out, I changed the name to 3W. I never liked to keep anything the same for long. To my satisfaction I got a review in one of the key alternative publishing magazines of the time. This was a densely written American magazine that listed hundreds of the most arcane and fascinating fanzines and alternative magazines put out around the world. It was a great read in its own right. They covered the newly renamed 3W magazine in the Technology section, and I couldn't have asked for a better understanding of what I was trying to do.

" **Global Networking Newsletter Vol 1, #2, December 1993.** "

Netsurfers, this is it! This is the map to the Internet. Get it, turn to the back pages, where each issue has a list of utterly crucial files available via ftp, gopher or WWW, and just go do it. But 3W is more than just a list of neat stuff. There's articles on how to get stuff, and detailed information and samples of neat stuff. There's more neat stuff here than the Archie McPhee Catalog. Even though 3W is written at a level that an average Net user can understand, there's stuff here for absolute newbie and NetGod as well. I actually used an article from issue #2 for my real job. No shit!

The article "Destination Russia" was extremely valuable in getting information about getting the

Russian operation online, an bypassing the incredibly unreliable phone system that plagues xUSSR. And there's a look at the most interesting VR/VC experiment happening - the Virtual City. 3W is the best printed guide to the Net that I've read.

FACTSHEET FIVE

And then I was listed as No.1 in Wired's list of High-tech and Electronic 'Zines.

"British 'zine that maps the far reaches of the Internet. Invaluable tips and access info. Written for the average net dweller."

WIRED 2.06 JUNE ISSUE

Despite the rapidly changing Internet scene and increasing interest from the outside world, after a couple of issues of 3W I was in a bit of a rut. I was also broke.

Producing the magazine was a lot of work and I didn't really have the momentum to keep doing everything all on my own, a pattern I later came to recognise well. I loved the set-up period, the drama of inventing a product, of naming it and making it into a real thing, but the moment it was real I lose interest. It is attention deficit writ large, the combination of insight, vision and the desire to find new stimulation that will keep you from tending to a project over the long term. At the time I knew none of this. I was just feeling restless and anxious.

The web was also taking on a life of its own and I could see opportunities there. For me, doing something online was becoming more attractive than repeatedly creating a paper-based magazine. At the same time, I had to keep it going for a bit longer. I was waiting for something to turn up.

My old boss at Goldsmiths, Dave Riddle, ran an online group for people who worked with Apple Macs. I liked the community. I had come to understand the world of email lists and had run them myself. I liked meeting people who were interested in the same sort of things I was, and in things I had never thought of.

Dave organised a meet up for the members and I went along. I wasn't much of a networker but I liked to socialise. We met at the Pizza Express on Museum Street in central London. About twenty people turned up. I filed into the back room of the restaurant and sat at a long table with the others, who were mostly techies and computer people. They were mostly men. I was trapped. I didn't enjoy tech talk and was hemmed in. I wanted to talk about the Internet and my magazine. After I took my place a guy sat down opposite and grinned at me. He asked what I did. I told him, bashfully, that I produced a magazine called The World Wide Web Newsletter. His eyes widened.

'That's my bible,' he said. 'I keep it next to my computer.'

His name was Steve Bowbrick and he'd come out of the London College of Printing photography course, where he sometimes taught. He knew about magazine production and he knew designers. He knew more than me about a lot of things but I had the jump on the Internet.

I was such a loner and so isolated in Hackney that the thought that people actually

bought and enjoyed my mag came as a shock. We cha ed through the meal about the Internet. I told him about 3W, how I was getting on. I tried to disguise my growing boredom with the whole thing. Steve was smart and funny and by the end of the meal I asked him if he'd like to come and help me produce the next issue.

Steve was one of those people that, when you look back, come into your life as if guided by providence, at the right moment. His skill set complemented mine and extended it in various areas. We got on well, having a sense of humour and a liking for a drink in common. He lived in Bow over in East London, in an ex-council flat, I lived in Hackney in a small flat. We were typical of that era, arts graduates looking for a role, looking for a way to leverage what we knew of the past and what we were interested in without much of an idea of how to go about it.

He had one key attribute that seemed to be almost lacking in me: he knew how to collect useful people, he had a large circle of friends and acquaintances and he immediately put them at my disposal. More than that, we got on very well, we became good friends with a common outlook. Although we started off discussing the magazine, we really ranged over every subject under the internet and before long we were discussing what came next. I didn't know it yet, but I had found the person who would be my startup co-founder. The mission was accelerating.

Soon after Steve started to work with me on the magazine, in May 1994, I was invited to exhibit at the Internet World show in London. They offered me a free stand and I happily took it.

The show was owned by Alan Meckler, an American entrepreneur who owned various magazines and shows including Internet World magazine, but it was run in London by a small team, most of whom became lifelong friends. It was tiny by the standards that were to come, with a small roster of speakers.

It was held in the Novotel hotel in Hammersmith, West London. I didn't really have anything for the stand so I just took a pile of magazines and sold them to whoever was passing. I met a lot of people who would be important in the world that was about to develop. I stood on my stand for two days and sold copies of the magazine by the dozen, direct to people who had come to an internet show, who had an inkling of what was going on. For the first time I felt the power of what I was doing and heard from people who were desperate to find out what was going on.

As with many things that came later, my brother had introduced me a new technology — the mobile phone. On his bidding I went to a shop on Tottenham Court Road and signed up for my first contract, a tiny Sony phone, known to us as a 'Mars bar' because if its shape. I loved my phone but it was soon stolen from me. I left it on a pile of boxes at the Internet World show and, bang, it was gone. I felt it was emblematic that the future came together on that day, in that place. It held out both the promise and the threat of what was to come.

The first London Internet World was a poor show. The next year was better, and Alan Meckler asked me to be the Chair. It was all still very technical and most of the presenters in those early years were hard core technical people who had little interest in popular content. Rob Blokzijl (bless him, I spent a couple of years with him much later on sitting on the Nominet board. He never said a word) spoke on changes in the communications infrastructure in central and eastern Europe. Gail Markham who discussed the UNOM project which has produced a 34 Mbps ATM cross connect and Felix van Rijn from Holland spoke on the typology of electronic services and critical factors for adoption and use of electronic services.

None of these people actually believed in or really knew anything about an IP based Internet. There were some interesting people at the show, including the now legendary Chris Locke who is now incarnated as RageBoy who wrote the Cluetrain Manifesto (or did he go mad, it's hard to tell) but was then General Manager, Internet Group, Mecklermedia. I never saw him, to my eternal pity, because I didn't actually have a pass to the conference. Despite being an exhibitor at the show, they wouldn't let me in.

On my way back I got off the tube at Kings Cross in north London to catch a bus back home to Hackney. As I came out from the tube I saw a newspaper sign, *John Smith Dead*.

John Smith was the leader of the Labour party who, after eighteen years of Conservative rule, was on course to win power in the next election. At 8.05 a.m. that morning in his Barbican flat he had suffered a heart a ack. His wife phoned an ambulance and he was rushed to St Bartholomew's Hospital but died at 9.15. He never regained consciousness. His death opened the way to Tony Blair to take control of the Labour Party and, a few years later, to win power in a landslide, but I knew none of that as I stood outside the station on that day. It seemed like a terrible tragedy. From that day, the growing Internet and the New Labour project started to run in some sort of parallel.

10

Birth of the CyberCafé

1994

ARPANET/Internet celebrates 25th anniversary

Communities begin to be wired up directly to the Internet

Shopping malls arrive on the Internet

Arizona law firm of Canter & Siegel"spams" the Internet with email advertising green card lottery services; Net citizens flame back

NSFNET traffic passes 10 trillion bytes/month

Yes, it's true - you can now order pizza from the Hut online

WWW edges out telnet to become 2nd most popular service on the Net (behind ftp-data) based on % of packets and bytes traffic distribution on NSFNET

First Virtual, the first cyberbank, open up for business

After noticing that many network software vendors used domain.com in their documentation examples, Bill Woodcock and Jon Postel register the domain.

RFC 1605: SONET to Sonnet Translation

RFC 1607: A VIEW FROM THE 21ST CENTURY

[HOBBES' INTERNET TIMELINE]

And then I invented something truly new in the world.

An organisation called Artec contacted me and told me they had promised an internet event for a weekend seminar, Towards the Aesthetics of the Future an arts weekend at the Institute of Contemporary Arts (ICA) in London, March 12-13, 1994. Their problem was, they didn't know what an internet event might be. I had, of course, played the ICA with Loophole Cinema and it had showcased the start of Damien Hirst's career. To me it was hallowed ground.

They asked if I'd be interested in doing something for them. They had a budget of five hundred pounds. I did have an idea. I'd been reading about an online cafe, in San Francisco, called SFnet Coffeehouse Network which had been started in July 1991 by a man called Wayne Gregori. In his cafes you could use a coin in the slot machine to pay for dial up time on a bulletin board. I loved the idea but thought it would be better to use a real internet connection. I saw this offer as my chance and I took artist Heath Bunting who was interested in the online world to have a look at the theatre space at the ICA.

With my mind working overtime, in the epiphany stage of an idea, I imagined a cafe setup with computers connected to the internet on each table, with menus setting out what you could do and waiting staff to help you navigate the online world. As we stood at the door to the theatre a name popped into my head: Cybercafe. It was a good name, it did what it said on the tin.

I wrote up my idea and pitched it to them. This is what I wrote.

Relax online with a cappuccino and chat around the world. Explore the global Internet from the comfort of our coffee bar. Log on to the best conversation from around the world.

The CyberCafé will introduce you to the Information Superhighway. For two days only, Artec brings the Internet to the ICA. Visitors to TtAofF94 will be able to browse the Internet using state of the art Apple Mac software.

Choose from a menu of Internet tools - help and advice will be on hand from the Café staff.

Regular workshops and presentations will run throughout the weekend. Check out the CyberCafé

World Wide Web server for multimedia information. Talk live to artists around the world via Internet Relay Chat; send and receive e-mail; search the global databanks with TurboGopher; find software and information files for your collection using Fetch and Archie; read the News with NewsWatcher; Finger famous people across the world; log on to mind-bending MOOS and play your life away.

Installing a CyberCafé

In order to introduce visitors to the highways and byways of the Internet during TtAotF94 I would like to install a 'CyberCafé'. This would consist of Apple Macs with 14.4baud modem links to the Internet. All the Macs would carry a suite of Internet software: Mosaic (World Wide Web); Homer (Internet Relay Chat); Eudora (e-mail); TurboGopher (Gopher servers and Veronica searches); Fetch (anonymous FTP servers); NewsWatcher (Usenet news); Finger (finger); Telnet (line-based services, e.g., MOOS). Each Mac would have its own phone line to allow Internet connection via Demon.

The CyberCafé would have various net components apart from the ICA event: a CyberCafé World Wide Web server; a CyberCafé Internet Relay Chat channel during the event; a mail address for the event; links to other art and creative network sites before and during the event.

Artec commissioned the event and the ICA put a lot of effort into making it happen. There was no Internet access at the gallery of course and we had to open up the phone system so we could plug a bunch of modems into it. It was challenging, but I had met a geeky technician called Ferghas Mackay who was working with Demon Internet and he helped assemble a lot of the project. I was in my element, at the ICA again with a cutting-edge project that straddled the world of art and technology. As usual, I massively over promised for the event, forgetting that everybody a ending would, almost by definition, have no idea what all this meant or why they might want it.

We borrowed a pile of modems and Macs and set up on white plastic tables with browsers and IRC clients and no doubt Gopher etc. It was a great success and I hugely enjoyed doing it, though I spent most of my time in the bar.

The day was successful, a lot of people came along and tried out the connections, but it ended in chaos. There was a live link-up via a chat program to BANFF in Canada where there was another conference going on but I was too lazy or disorganised to create new logins for everyone present. They all ended up logging in as me which made for an incredibly confused (yet hilarious) conversation. I'm not sure the ICA were impressed, but I was. A new world had just opened up.

From the Cybercafe event came my first attempt at starting a real company. My cofounder was Ferghas Mackay who did much of the technical work to make the Cybercafe happen and who I'd got on with really well. We called it interSPACE Internet Information Publishing. I thought we were going to start a business to get people onto the internet, but our relationship blew up a few weeks after the event when I discovered he had been hired for some work directly as a result of the Cybercafe event, work that I felt should have come to the new company. At the time I didn't understand how he could cheat me, and I felt terrible about it, but looking back I realise that it was just a job to him, he was an eager puppy so he said yes. It stopped any chance of developing a business.

That first attempt at a company exists now only as a sad footnote on the yellowing press release from the first Cybercafe event where it says: *These pages have been assembled by interSPACE Internet Information Publishing.* I had strong ideas about how an internet company should proceed and InterSPACE set the hare running, but it quickly died.

My prediction of 'good press coverage all round' for the Cybercafe event didn't exactly pan out, but it eventually led to something even better. Only Jack Schofield, the Guardian's technology journalist (who is still going strong in the same role) mentioned the event, but his tiny reference had huge ramifications.

Like superhighway hitchhikers in Seattle and San Francisco, London's Interneterati may soon be able to hang out in a computer cafe, mocha in one hand, mouse in the other.[4]

This mention led to a sequence of events that eventually broke me through into an actual nascent internet industry. Heath told Schofield that he was going to open *'a Soho Cybercafe offering terminals with 24-hour free Internet access alongside caffeine and sandwiches'.* I hadn't discussed opening Cybercafes with Heath. Although the idea of a commercial cafe had surfaced briefly, but I was convinced that the Web itself was becoming a reality and I had a bunch of ideas of what to do with it, but I wanted to work with Steve Bowbrick. The InterSPACE fiasco had given me an idea. Soon we seemed to have sparked a small cybercafe war and the Guardian wrote about a challenger to Heath's project.

'They could still be pipped to the post if the ECafe, a rival venture conceived by a Cambridge physics student, is realised before the end of the year.[5]'

The ECafe was thought up by Mark Cheverton and he talked of a Camden cafe with sixteen terminals loaded with Mosaic *'the widely lauded killer application'.* In the way that the internet itself would soon accelerate all new ideas, mutating and spreading them around the world, in this case the traditional press under-took the same service. Eventually, through the grapevine, Heath heard about a company starting a real internet cafe. They were proposing to call it Cybercafe. In anger he posted a threat to them, telling them that they could not use 'our' name for their business. The Guardian followed up the story.

Founders Keith Teare and David Rowe have taken the name Cybercafe Ltd for the company that will operate the establish-ment. This has irritated Heath Bunting, who had hoped to estab-lish an eatery called Cybercafe in Soho's Bateman Street. Bunting has complained that 'these people are government agents'.[6]

Heath was a subversive artist who was given to pranks and in-terventions, and it's hard to know whether he had ever seriously considered opening a cafe, but I assumed this would be the end of it. Steve stepped in and played the role of peacemaker, offer-ing to meet the founders and find out what they were doing. He came back and reported that they were altogether very pleasant, they had started an Internet service provider called Easynet and had a whole office block on Whitfield Street in the centre of Lon-don, near Tottenham Court Road.

'You should go and meet them,' he said. I was embarrassed by Heath's behaviour, but also not really sure about these interlop-ers, so I went for a visit and found a gang of four: Eva Pascoe, Gene Teare, Keith Teare and David Rowe. They had a corner building near the Tottenham Court Road.

Cyberia took advantage of the premises that Easynet had leased, which included a large corner shop front and basement that the ISP didn't need. Between them these four entrepreneurs, who came from a variety of business, academic and political backgrounds, quickly built and opened the first commercial internet cafe in the world. The explosion of this form was about to begin.

The cafe was actually the project of the women, Eva Pascoe and Gene Teare, the partners of Rowe and Teare. They planned a cybercafe for women only as a feminist education and campaigning space.

David Rowe was a small time entrepreneur in computers and databases. He had met Keith Teare, who was largely a political activist at the time, and they had fallen to discussing opportunities. They had ended up deciding to start an ISP and this had led to Easynet and the premises on Whitfield Street. Gene was a South African activist who had met Keith through politics and Eva was an academic working at the LSE. Because the building they rented for Easynet had shop premises on the ground floor, they had decided to use it to open an internet cafe for women only as an education resource. In this way businesses were started at that time and the world was changed. They had certainly heard of my project as their first intention was to use the name Cybercafe for their project and they registered the name Cybercafe Limited on August 19th, 1994. Following Heath's intervention, they changed their minds and came up with the name Cyberia, which became the world famous first internet cafe.

When I visited them they told me they also had a basement and would be interested in Steve and I moving in. I thought it was a great idea and they became my landlords.

Heath was later instrumental in creating a real anarchic hack space, Backspace, which flourished in Clink Street for just under four years, closing just before the millennium. Backspace was everything that Cyberia didn't become, though they both had a lot in common and both took advantage of a moment when nobody had internet access at home and anything seemed possible.

Long afterwards, when internet cafes had spread to every corner of the world, Teju Cole wrote,

'One sign of the newly vital Nigerian economy and one of the most apparent, is the proliferation of Internet cafes. There had been none when I left home. Now there are several in every neighbourhood, and there must be hundreds in Lagos alone[7].'

I brought the Internet cafe into the world. It was a synthesis out of my own observations, something that could only come from immersion in the world that I had discovered. It spread like wildfire. I was proud, though nobody much cared how it had originated. Like the best new things, like memes, it was simple to understand, offered value to those who used it and carried a reason for its own dissemination. My best ideas were like real memes — those that were not, that were missing one or more parts of the equation, withered quickly on the vine. Sometimes others were quick to pick them up.

Despite the debacle of InterSPACE, I was sure there was need for a web company. I started to think about what that meant and how to invent the next phase. I was fed up with running a magazine. It wasn't that it made no money and circulation was static, it was that I could see that the Web was starting to become a real thing and I was desperate to do something in that space.

Steve and I had been mulling over starting a web company, even though no such thing existed. Our planning involved sitting around in a Soho café called The Living Room and talking about what was going on and what might come next and how we could get ourselves bootstrapped into business. We both had mobile phones by then and felt like we were inventing a new way of working. We were making a startup, though nobody had ever heard of that term. Although there were a few other internet companies that we had met, we didn't think we were part of anything bigger than ourselves.

I had seen how a few businesses were starting their own web sites but it was obvious that these were being built by enthusiastic amateurs, technicians and programmers within companies who were more or less freelancing the work. The sites were badly designed (if they were designed at all) and unimaginative. Although the web was so new that almost anything was better than nothing, I could see that a more structured approach to site development would soon be necessary, and I believed I could sell this concept to companies. I came up with the idea of building a team to professionalise the process of building web sites — to bring in designers and project managers, to create structure and process. What I wanted to do was create a product that we could sell to companies. The Web was now growing fast and internet access was becoming more widely available, it seemed it would only be a matter of time before the Web was a normal part of everyday business.

We decided we wanted to start a proper company and went looking for offices. The only place we looked at was a small room in a block on Curtain Road in Shoreditch. At the time this was about as far from trendy as it was possible to get and the office cost £76 a week. We knew there was no way we could afford it, even if we wanted to leave the centre of London, which we didn't.

I knew Hoxton Square from my art life. Although we could barely afford it, we would sometimes end up at jazz club The Bass Clef, which later turned into the Blue Note. It was an island of culture in something of a dark desert. The jazz magazine, Straight No Chaser, printed by the same people who were producing 3W, was based on the square.

The partner of Bea from Loophole had a flat in the top of an old building on Rivington Street where we sometimes hung out. It was the sort of post-industrial place that we loved and artists were starting to make it home, it was cheap and fairly empty. Loophole investigated an empty power station as a potential event site, later it became home to the National Centre for Circus Arts, exactly the sort of crossover that we loved. But the internet was not yet a force and there were no startups in the area. The White Cube gallery wouldn't move there for another six years, although various YBAs were starting to move in to the area. Gary Hume and Sarah Lucas had squatted there years before and Alexander McQueen would take up residence on the square. The highest profile events, still tiny compared with what was to come, were Joshua Compston's crazy village fair pastiches, A Fete Worse Than Death, which attracted artists such as Damien Hirst to exhibit art and penises. The conversion of Shoreditch to a real estate boom town was still a few years off.

We nearly become the first internet residents of Shoreditch which would have been the crossover between my art world and my internet world made flesh, but it never happened.

During my meeting with the Easynet founders following Heath's intervention, I told them about my plans. They said they had a basement under the shop and would be happy to rent to us. Steve came along and we haggled a rent — five hundred pounds a week. The basement was empty, open and sparse. It had been used as a wine merchant's cellar and was decorated with barrel lids and pictures of grapes. We assumed we would have the whole thing, but David soon sent a builder down to make a wall along the middle, and our new company started its life in an enclosed space with windows to look out onto the rest of the basement.

Easynet had set up in the offices on the top floors and they had a leased internet connection from Pipex, which was a huge rarity in those days. The entire bandwidth of their connection was 64k, which they were using for their ISP and for the internet cafe that they had built out on the ground floor. As part of our rent they rant a line of ethernet down to the basement, put a terminator on the end and told us we were welcome to plug our computers into it, 'but please don't take the terminator off or the whole network will go offline'. We didn't know anything about internet bandwidth, but we soon learnt that a 64k connection didn't really provide much to work with, but for the first months of our precarious new existence, it changed our lives.

Years later, Keith Teare wrote in his blog

> *When I helped start EasyNet in 1994 there were only 2 ISPs in the UK. It cost us $50,000 to start the company. Becoming an ISP was suddenly within reach of 2 guys and a credit card. Today, with Video and Voice over IP technology it will soon be possible to start a communications company for less that $50,000. This is going to make competing with the big telcos an achievable goal for many startups. Somebody is going to become the UUNet of communications, and the Earthlink of communications and even the AOL of communications. Many thousands of others will become local communications service providers, just as there are thousands of local ISPs.*

He told me another story at the time. While Dave Rowe set up the business side of the startup, he was responsible for developing the technical side. Pushed for time and eager to launch their service as quickly as possible, he hadn't worked out a way to drop the modem lines after each call. They built a walk in cupboard in the corner of the ground floor space, effectively in the corner of Cyberia, and connected each of the modems there to a phone line and to their Pipex internet connection.

'For the first few days,' he told me, 'I had to sit in that cupboard and reset each modem as soon as someone put the phone down.'

Without this manual intervention they would soon have had no dial-up lines available. That was the reality of internet startups — you hacked what you needed to hack and if you couldn't do it with technology you did it with your finger.

Issue four of 3W was the end of the project. There was too much else happening and I had run out of money. The final issue had the only full colour cover, using an image from an article Sean Clark wrote about virtual reality. Steve wrote about emoney and Heath put together a huge listing of online fanzines. Internet for Dummies had come out, showing that the world was recognising our baby. We offered a pair of modems which had been donated by US Robotics and a copy of Internet Unleashed, the first thousand-page Internet book, for which I had written the World Wide Web chapter.

The bigger truth was, though, that I could see the Web itself was becoming viable as a medium and I wanted to get involved and try out some ideas. First, I had to find a way out of the paper publishing world.

The internet was coming to the attention of the wider world fast now and the commercial potential was not missed by traditional publishers. Since the release of The Whole Internet User's Guide and Catalog a couple of years before, a flood of books was starting to hit the market and many of them were now sent to my home address for review. I came home one day to find a whole sack of books had been delivered.

I chose a few to review, including one called The Canadian Internet Handbook which had hit the top of the sales charts in

Canada. This gave me the idea that I should write a similar book about the UK internet scene. I got in touch, rather randomly, with Prentice Hall and they jumped at the chance. Within a few months I had a contract to write Internet UK. By the time I came to write it 3W was over and I was working between .net magazine and Webmedia. Somehow I had to find time to write a book about the internet alongside everything else.

11

Future .net

The Web had become a reality and I wanted to be part of it. I was wondering what to do with 3W when a guy called Steve Carey phoned the Webmedia office out of the blue, suggesting a meeting. I had no idea who he was, but I was excited and went down to Bath to meet him at their Bath campus. He told me that they were going to start a proper consumer internet magazine and blow 3W away. Would I like to come and join them on their project?

3W was more or less moribund. I had just about lost interest in publishing a magazine and the thought of doing another issue filled me with dread. At the same time, the things I had been writing about were multiplying and there was a growing audience who almost knew what I was talking about. The interesting commercial public elements of the internet were multiplying almost by the day. Although Steve and I had moved on to a Web company, were fascinated by what was happening and knew we were at the centre of something. We were determined to stay there as the land rush developed.

At the meeting in Bath they told me they were going to start an internet magazine. A real one. I found that the idea was the brainchild of Stuart Anderton who had been active on the CIX bulletin board and had watched the Demon proposal take flight. He knew that something big was brewing and he'd persuaded Carey to take a risk on a consumer internet magazine. They found me through 3W. They needed someone with internet magazine experience, and nobody in the country had it except for me and they wanted to launch, fast.

My desire to be responsible for a whole magazine had withered on the vine but the idea of being part of a proper commercial magazine from a real publisher, and getting paid real money for it, was attractive. It wasn't just the money, though I could see it would come in very handy to get Webmedia off the ground. The meeting went well and I liked the Future guys and I liked that they wanted me. I thought I'd give it a go. The only problem was that I didn't want to move out of London. This came as a shock to them. They were Future fanboys, they were having the time of their lives, doing fun stuff and being paid for it. Just what I wanted to do, only I just didn't want to do it in Bath. I haggled the salary up and told them they would have to send me to the World Wide Web conference that was coming up in Chicago. They didn't seem bothered by these demands, so I signed up for a six-month stint.

With these guys I had a problem that came to define my business career, although I never really identified it, let alone resolved it. I sat with people who wanted what I had. I had proved myself by getting up and making a magazine when nobody else was even thinking of it. I got a jump on the world, and I did it off my own bat from my little flat in Hackney. To me that was embarrassing, but to outsiders it looked fairly amazing. I was never at ease in these sorts of meetings. I wanted what was on offer, I knew how to haggle, but I had a lack of self confidence in my own ability. I was learning to step up, but it would take some time and cause a lot of problems along the way.

Future was founded by a charismatic guy called Chris Anderson who later became famous for starting the TED talks. He became successful off the back of inventing the cover disk for magazines. Anderson started with a magazine called Amstrad Action in 1985, and he was the first to put free software on the cover. This innovation gave him explosive growth and by the time I came along they had moved all their publications to Bath (after a companywide vote), creating a sort of campus feel to the town centre. They had offices all around the town and their numerous staff all knew each other, socialised together and even looked much the same. They tended to move around from publication to publication within the group, a bit like a Google of Facebook campus. They attracted the ambitious and the innovative. Future relationships and marriages were fairly common.

In the campus they had the knowledge to quickly launch a very professional magazine — that was really their prime product - but they lacked internet expertise. Stuart told me that they had an editor and were going to launch, and would I like to move down to Bath and join them. I thought this was a non-starter, partly because I still felt that I'd only recently got established in London but also because I didn't really want to work with a paper magazine. I was keen to get Webmedia started with Steve and we'd only just moved into our new office. On the other hand, I was intrigued by the idea of a real commercial internet mag. I told them all of this and they suggested that I work down in Bath for three months and then work remotely from London for another three. They would pay me handsomely, put me up in a bed and breakfast while I was in Bath. They also agreed to send me to a few Internet conferences that were coming up. In return for this I would help them assemble the content for a new magazine and write articles for them. I asked Steve what he thought and he told me to go for it, so I agreed to spend six months working on their project. By the beginning of October, I was driving up and down to Bath each week, leaving on Monday morning and coming back on Friday afternoon.

In Bath they put me up in a bed and breakfast which they paid for. I ate scrambled egg on toast for breakfast every morning. It was the first time in my life I'd been catered to and looked after and, although the place was a hellhole, it was a clean and tidy hellhole and I didn't have to pay for it. Future assembled a team to put the magazine together, that was their prime skill, and we started work. They announced that it was going to be called .net, which I thought was an excellent title. The editor was a guy called Matt Bielby and the deputy, who eventually became editor, was Richard Longhurst.

Future Publishing was based in Bath, and they almost occupied the centre of town like a campus. In the evenings the Future crowd filled the bars and no doubt after the pubs closed jumped into each others knickers. It was that sort of town, that sort of time. The deputy editor of .net, and lined up to become the editor before long, was Richard Longhurst. Richard sat in the corner looking like Morrisey from the Smiths. He kept up a running commentary of a lewd nature and was scathingly funny. Richard was Future through and through. He came from PC Format. Future were brilliant at launching titles, but they had no-one who knew anything about the Internet in 1994. I went down part time and stuck my oar in. I don't know if they appreciated it, but they paid me well and looked after me. I wrote for them for some time. Richard became a freelance and now runs Lovehoney, a hugely successful sex toy site which he started from his bedroom. Nothing about Richard would ever surprise me, and this least of all.

For the second issue of .net I offered to interview Eva and Gene and do an article on Cyberia. I thought it was an important part of the internet scene and wanted to tell the story of how it had come to be. I also thought it would be interesting to tell the readers of .net where things might go next. And, they were now my friends and landlords, though of course I didn't mention that in the article.

Cyberia was an interesting beast, part of a bigger Easynet project. It looked confident and reassuring on the outside but was in reality about as solid as my new company, Webmedia, which was at that point in residence in the basement but without an identity or customers.

After Cyberia launched, half the world decided that running an Internet cafe was a route to riches. Some started tiny local cafes, and the UK is still do ed with these combined internet access and coffee joints, which certainly enhance the neighbourhood and provide fast access for a large group of people. Others went the whole hog and invested in huge flashy premises with a lot of bells and whistles.

Future sent me to the Third World Wide Web conference, which took place in Chicago on the shores of a freezing lake. I had made sure this trip and another to Internet World in Washington was in the deal I had with them. The Third World Wide Web conference marked the start of the commercial web, even if most of the participants didn't realise it. Mosaic had just been released and Tim Berners-Lee spoke at the event. It was still a very academic show with just a few small stands offering semi-commercial products.

By the time the event came up we had a sample copy of .net which would be a ached to hundreds of thousands of other Future magazines as a sample. I took a box of these samples to the conference and located a table which had various internet service leaflets laid out on it. I opened the top of the box and walked swiftly away. I thought I would get called to account for a blatantly commercial offering and wasn't willing to stay and risk embarrassment. I thought people might hate the mag. I needn't have worried — when I returned half an hour later the box was empty.

Everyone loved our new mag. It was unique, a professional consumer magazine thrown into a space that was on the verge of an explosion.

By the middle of the 1990s I knew I had to make a decision and I knew which side I would come down on. The world was waking up to the internet. Not so much to the myriad infinite uses, the potential to create and publish and distribute and undermine, but to the inherent financial potential. I had to jump one way or another. I was still technically in Loophole Cinema, just about. I still had a studio, just about. But the business side beckoned and I was entering its thrall. I had seen the future. I had taken to wearing suits, shirts, ties, all the time, all day every day. I had found a home, a niche where I was taken seriously and where, to my surprise, I seemed to be a bit ahead of the curve. Ahead of the curve, in those marvellous shimmering accelerating days when nobody knew anything, that was something to treasure. Even the best business brains, especially the best business brains, were behind that curve. It was my time and bliss it was that very morn to be alive.

I was made, in many ways, for business. Not for the graft of management or the day-to-day slog of hitting targets. I didn't even know what a target was and I never learnt to read the profit and loss account. I had found in the creative drive that business offered a way forward, a method of leveraging resources, of creating the means to accumulate resources and to do with them what I would. It was a different world, but maybe not so different.

It wasn't so easy to leave art. I had joined a cult and had internalised its rules and routines. I expected my reward in this temporal place, not in heaven and I could not just shuck off the best self-definition I had ever constructed for myself. Punk had also been a cult, and the internet was fast becoming one, but art alone had wider validity and I was loathe to return to the real world. In addition, I really liked making art, I felt I was an artist, knew I was an artist. I decided I could not throw off the moniker, as several of my friends did, but had to stay loyal. The thing I was building, it was conceptual, the biggest and best conceptual work imaginable.

'Damien Hirst, eat your heart out, I'm coming after you', I thought. 'You have shown me the way.'

Then I abandoned myself to my commercial instinct.

12

Let a Thousand Flowers Bloom

1995

WWW surpasses ftp-data in March as the service with greatest traffic on NSFNet based on packet count, and in April based on byte count

Traditional online dial-up systems (CompuServe, America Online, Prodigy) begin to provide Internet access

Chris Lamprecht (aka "Minor Threat") becomes the first person banned from accessing the Internet by a US District Court judge in Texas

A number of Net related companies go public, with Netscape leading the pack with the 3rd largest ever NASDAQ IPO share value (9 August)

Registration of domain names is no longer free. Beginning 14 September, a $50 annual fee has been imposed.

Operation Home Front connects, for the first time, soldiers in the field with their families back home via the Internet. Richard White becomes the first person to be declared a muni-

tion, under the USA's arms export control laws, because of an RSA file security encryption program tattooed on his arm
(:wired496:)

RFC 1882: The 12-Days of Technology Before Christmas

Technologies of the Year: WWW, Search engines

Emerging Technologies: Mobile code (JAVA, JAVAscript), Virtual environments (VRML), Collaborative tools

Hacks of the Year: The Spot (Jun 12), Hackers Movie Page (12 Aug)

[HOBBES' INTERNET TIMELINE]

" '*A new breed of Internet artist and entrepreneur* "
is emerging. They have, in effect, created a new job for the nineties, a new industry and a cultural renaissance. Take Goldsmiths graduate, Ivan Pope, who runs a company called Webmedia. It specialises in creating "magazines" for clients on the World Wide Web, the user friendly part of the Internet. Founded less than a year ago with former media lecturer Steve Bowbrick, Webmedia's turnover is already £500,000 and it employs seven people. The atmosphere in the London office is laid back, to say the least: a giant stereo plays ambient music, while young men sit at their computers and smoke roll-ups.'

TOM HODGKINSON, GUARDIAN, 1994

All through the first half of the nineties my art friends still assumed that I was going to stay in their orbit while it became more and more obvious to me that I would have to leave. As my business started to grow I supported everyone as best I could, but it became clear first to others and then to me that I was making my own way out in my own way. I kept a studio for years: after Temple Works I occupied subterranean spaces in Brick Lane, in the Trumans Brewery and then a vast damp railway arch in Hackney that cost me a huge amount but which I never used for anything. I was otherwise occupied, although the Webmedia diary notes occasionally, 'Ivan up his arch' in Steve's sardonic hand. I ended up in a clean dry council space in a converted industrial space behind my house in Hackney and from here I invested the money that had started to flow in digital technology and the storage of endless collected objects, but the game was over. When I applied for a postgraduate fine art degree at Goldsmiths the sneering of the visiting assessors was almost palpable, one not even deigning to stray from the door to look at anything. They were going through the motions, as I was, I guess. I had picked up painting again on huge found metal panels and on huge prints that my HP put out, but they seemed to only want the digital stuff, the Internet. 'Why are you painting?' they asked, and that was that.

At some point I had started to have offices instead of studios and the work that went on in those offices was done for the same reasons as the work in the studios, yet it occurred in a different planet at a different speed for a different audience. It would take me many years to escape from that environment.

On the eighteenth of August 1995 Steve Bowbrick and I started a company called Webmedia. At that moment we had our own world to ourselves to invent as we wished. It was a bubble but a bubble of the purest type. Now we had the space to create our own vision of the world. Everything I had done up to now seemed to fit into this bubble: the years of punk, the drama and the do-it-yourself ethic, the excitement and discoveries of art and how Hirst himself had set out to become a business and now, layered on top, the internet itself, an embryonic and barely usable system that seemed to hold the greatest potential, a mix of everything that I loved.

We had been hanging about in London with our mobile phones trying to work out what to do next. 3W magazine had been dying on its feet and I had been in Bath working on the launch of .net magazine. The web had moved on a bit. It was looking like a real thing. The excitement was palpable. I said I wanted to professionalise the business of making web sites. At that point what sites there were built by the resident tech and looked dreadful.

I said the web is a medium, not a technology. I said, beneath the pavement, the internet. We both said, it's the internet, stupid! That autumn, as my enforced exile in Bath drew to an end, we started looking around for premises. We examined an office in Curtain Road, around the corner from Hoxton Square, but decided we couldn't afford the rent. Then Steve made friends with the people who were starting their own Internet café, Cyberia, and they offered us their basement as offices. They told us they had rented the entire building for their new internet service provider, Easynet, but they had no use for the ground floor or basement. They had decided to put an Internet café on the ground floor but we could rent part of the basement. We moved in around October. I don't know what we thought we were doing. We had no money, no equipment, no plan and the basement was an empty shell. It had previously been used by a wine distributor and the décor reflected that: dodgy thin red carpet and wooden barrel lids on the walls. David Rowe, one of the founders of Easynet, arranged to have the basement cleared out. Although we were only renting half of it there was initially no wall so we sat in a huge open space.

The ISP and the café both ran off a tiny 64k internet connection that was distributed around the building by a cable setup called Ethernet. Every computer had its own connector to the network from a main cable which ran throughout the building. When we moved in they ran an extension to the cable down into the basement and put a terminating plug on the end.

'Don't take this off,' they admonished. 'You'll bring the entire operation to a halt.'

So, for the first six months of our existence we shared this tiny connection to the internet with everyone upstairs and all Easynet's external customers. It was heaven.

Just as my life was getting very complicated I got a call from a head-hunter. It was the first and, I am sure, the last such call I ever got, but it was exciting. The hunter was looking for someone to run Sky's satellite-based internet service. I imagine that, given a brief that probably sounded like science fiction, someone had done a search of press cuttings and come up with my name. It was similar to when we started to hire people for Webmedia: who did you look for when nobody had ever done anything like this before?

The inquiry came right out of left field. It was the sort of job which I never knew existed and which I would never have applied for, but I was tempted. I talked to Steve about it. 'Should I go and do the interview?' I asked him. It was like going off to start a magazine with Future or working for Time Out, I always felt guilty about moonlighting but Steve never minded what I did. I said I'd go for an interview, so I put on my suit and trucked off to West London to Sky's headquarters at Osterley. The prospect was daunting — it was a huge corporate building in a field on the edge of town. I don't remember much of the interview except that I was fascinated as to how internet over satellites would work. Unfortunately, the guy I was talking to had no idea either. I might have laughed at the idea. I never heard anything from them again.

We moved our own Apple Macs From home into the space and constructed desks from trestles that we found in the basement and doors that we bought from the local builders' merchants. We sat on bags of cement in an office that resembled a crazy building site. We plugged into the Ethernet and bought a two-line phone system. Suddenly we had real internet connectivity which was on 24 hours a day. There was no dial up, no modem noises, no waiting for a line. We were encountering the future and it was clear that this type of access had a major impact on how we saw the internet, how we used it and what we could dream up.

'Do you think everyone will have this access?' we asked each other tentatively. It seemed impossible.

We quickly worked out our roles. It seemed important to define what we were doing, who we were, and to find some actual work. Steve started to read the media press and started making calls: you need a website; your project needs a website. It was remarkable, we had hit a golden moment. The people he was calling had heard of the internet and had a vague feeling that they should be doing something about it. Steve's calls were often the catalyst for action and within a few hours they would be in our makeshift office, discussing websites.

Soon we had the managing directors of serious and sensible media companies sitting on our cement sacks. We were in business.

I started sloganizing. I had a very strong sense of what we should be doing. 'We need to professionalise the web,' I told everyone I could get to listen. 'Web sites are being built by the techies, the systems operators, the guys who know about the web and are interested in it.'

I told everyone this was the wrong way around and that we needed to professionalise the industry. I made this up. I knew nothing about agencies. I could see though that there were various skill sets that could usefully be brought to bear on a web project. Designers was an obvious one, but I also wanted to add project managers and coders and others, to take a team approach to making a web site. Most of all I wanted them to stop looking horrible, to bring some elegance to commercial sites.

'Get the people who have budgets,' I told Steve. We went after companies in the television world, in film and advertising. 'They'll understand what a proper budget is,' we told each other in the pub after work. They would, but it would be a hard struggle to get them to hand them over.

As the idea for a web business turned from dream to reality, I took some radical and art slogans and adapted them for use by Webmedia. I was intrigued by a Paris 68 slogan, Beneath the pavement the beach, which I took to mean that by ripping up the paving blocks to riot you liberated yourself by finding the beach, if only metaphorically. I converted this to the slogan, Beneath the pavement the Internet. We also borrowed Bill Clinton's phrase, It's the economy, stupid and changed it to It's the Internet, Stupid. But the thing that worked the best was a Maoist slogan that we used straight up. 'Let a thousand flowers bloom' is a common misquotation of Chairman Mao Zedong's Let a hundred flowers blossom. The slogan was used during six weeks in the summer of 1957 when the Chinese intelligentsia were invited to criticize the political system then obtaining in Communist China. They were then imprisoned or killed. Not that that was my intent. I just liked the idea of a thousand different ideas blossoming, that seemed to describe what we were trying to achieve with Webmedia and we had some huge panels made up with a loud design and this slogan. We used it at shows for years. Nobody ever questioned the slogan or asked why we were using the propaganda of a man who killed millions, they just thought it was pretty cool. Mike had made us look cool and it was probably due in large part to his creativity that we quickly became some sort of poster boys for the new world of web design.

After doing a deal with Easynet, Steve and I moved ourselves into the basement at Whitfield Street. My white Russian godmother, Nina, always generous to me, had given me five thousand pounds for my birthday. It was the most she ever gave me. This surprise gift allowed me to propose that we start the business properly. Steve borrowed an equivalent amount from his parents and, after forming Webmedia Limited, we went to open a bank account. We chose at random the Midland Bank on Tottenham Court Road, and we took them up on their offer of a year's free banking so long as we didn't turnover above £100,000. Of course, we soon shot through this amount and started to pay fees, but for some reason the bank manager always hated us. We couldn't work it out, we thought that as we were a successful new company we must be what the bank wanted, but they were never less than horrible to us. In the end we assumed it was because they couldn't understand what we were doing and it scared them.

Steve brought along a young designer, Mike Bennett , who he had met at the London College of Printing. Like every single other designer in the world at that time, Mike knew nothing about the internet or the web, but he was a brilliantly skilled designer. From my experience of designing 3W myself I knew that I was hopeless as a designer so I was more than pleased to find we had a real one in the house. We did a deal with Mike. In return for a desk and working space in our office he would do the design work on any jobs we got. Of course, we would pay him for this, but it got us over the startup quandary of skill shortages.

We didn't have any furniture or equipment so we just picked up our own computers from home and took them with us. Steve insisted that the best way to make desks was to use door blanks from a diy shop, so we started building desks in this fashion, using some trestles we found in the basement. We connected to the internet while Mike designed our first brochures.

After a period of struggle, we got our first contract. Steve had made friends with a young guy in a huge record company, BMG. He started discussing projects with him. We were running fast in getting the word out. Mike had designed our first brochures, a glorious orange number in the style of the 90s, all clashing run together fonts. I made up the mad text and listed a number of interesting web sites which people came to think we had built. It wasn't deliberate deception, but it helped. Our landlords, Easynet and the Cyberia internet cafe, built a wall across the basement and cut our space down a lot while making it habitable and cosy. We were still working off tables placed across trestles, a concept that Steve insisted upon having read about it in Wired magazine.

Despite being reasonably frugal, we started to run through the money we had put up to start the business very quickly. There was rent to pay, we had mobile phones and we drew small amounts to keep our personal lives above water. One evening we went off to the pub for our usual working board meeting. When we got back to our basement there was an envelope sitting on Steve's keyboard addressed to Webmedia. Inside was a cheque for sixteen thousand pounds, the first instalment of our first web project: the building of a website for a band called Spiritualised. An energy rippled through the office — we knew we were on our way.

The contract to build a web site was a huge step forward. The problem was, we didn't really know how to build one. Steve and I were not designers or computer nerds. We knew a lot, but it was mostly theoretical, not practical. The arrival of a high-profile project meant we had to knuckle down to the next stage in double quick time.

We decided to recruit two more members of staff. This in itself was a huge leap into the dark and presented its own problems. Nobody had ever recruited for a web company before and we weren't at all sure who we would find. There was no option to look for people with experience, to attract rising stars in the industry. We would have to do what we spent the next few years doing — attract smart people who were interested in the space and hope they got up to speed quickly. We invented a couple of job titles and bought advertising space in The Guardian media section.

The truth was in those early days that we had no idea how to build a web site. Nobody did, not a single person in the entire world had done what we were attempting to do. Of course, there were plenty of people who had built web sites, and some of them were very good at it, but our mission was different. We were setting out to manage the process of putting a company on the web. I understood this, I knew it instinctively, it had been the basis of my desire to form Webmedia and I thought it was our mission. What I'd underestimated was the sheer amount of support that just didn't exist. There were no frameworks for making web sites, there was no web server software, no toolkits, no open-source software. Every project had to start again from scratch. You couldn't hire someone who would come with experience, who had tried and tested various approaches. There were no professional bodies, no documentation, no publications about making web sites. We could hire enthusiastic, skilled and knowledgeable designers and technicians, but their expertise was in an old world, not the world we wanted to create.

We were on our own, but the enormous void that surrounded us never figured in our calculations. How could it? We never would have embarked on such a dangerous project if we'd been the sort to sit down and think through all the ramifications. This was probably what gave us a head start on all the other people who would enter the industry over the next few years, who would turn out to be better and smarter and faster and more avaricious than us, we simply had no idea what we were doing.

Of course, it wasn't any longer just me on my own with a vision and an excitement. The internet was leaking out into the wider commercial world and week by week, day by day, even hour by hour, more people were noticing that something was happening. A huge avalanche, a tsunami, was gathering up above us or out to sea. We couldn't see it yet, but we had felt the tremor that set it off and it was now inevitable that sooner or later it would envelop us all.

On March 29th 1996, BT finally launched a mass market internet service which with their usual imagination and verve they called BT Internet. It was a dial up service without much going for it, but the huge marketing muscle of BT and the fact that they were already in everyone's home as a fixed line provider meant they gave a huge fillip to the connection industry. For many people it was the first time they could send email, transfer files and use the internet's vast resources. At that time the average Internet customer got 2.5Mb of web space and used a 33.6Kbps modem.

One of the first manifestations of this wider commercial interest in the internet was a flood of books that arrived on my doorstep that winter. First a few would come in ones and twos, then several each week and finally the postman dumped a sack of books on my Hackney stoop.

Among these books, most of which I looked at briefly and then put on my groaning shelves, I found a slim strangely shaped book called The Canadian Internet Guide. It had been published by Prentice Hall in Canada and it explained the internet for a Canadian audience. The thing that made me notice it was that it was a smash hit in Canada, rising to the top of the book charts. That set me wondering and with my idea-driven brain on I realised that there was scope for a similar book about the British internet scene.

I knew absolutely nothing about books publishing and how it worked so, using my sometime strangely reductionist mind I got in touch with Prentice Hall in London and asked them if they'd like a book about the internet. They had obviously been reading the same runes as a lot of other people because they certainly did want my UK internet book. Wishing a month or so I had a contract and a book outline. Then the realisation hit me: I actually had to write this book and write it in the midst of an increasingly crazy workload onto which I was frantically piling more and more things. Nevertheless, I started writing my first book and, with a fair amount of fudge and scraping, I finished it more or less on time.

Apart from not having a clue what we were doing with the technical side of building web sites, we had no idea of how to start, run or fund a business. By a piece of luck, we got an accountant who stood us in good stead for the next few years. During the first weeks of setting up Webmedia the responsibility for managing the paperwork fell to me. Steve and I looked up accountants in Time Out small ads and went to see a woman in a small, overheated office above a row of shops in Chalk Farm. We signed up with her although she scared us and I could smell a sad scene as soon as we walked through the door. She gave us a lot of instructions, none of which did I have any idea of following, so I just started to ignore the paperwork that quickly began to pile up in our new office.

As was to become obvious over the next decade, this was about as bad a decision as could be made. While I could understand what was needed and was fully capable of working out how to set things in motion, I had no ability to deal with the paperwork. It turned out to be my Achilles' heel, though at that point nobody knew it, least of all me.

Mike's accountant, Andrew Riddington, came to visit in our new subterranean space and, on passing my desk, picked a tax demand from the top of the pile and asked if we had paid it. I said I hadn't, but that I would soon get around to it. Sensing the quiet desperation in my voice he asked, 'Would you like me to help?' he said, and I could have fallen into his arms. From that moment we found we had acquired a key part of the Webmedia team — an accountant who could keep on top of everything that moved and who also called himself the best dressed accountant in town. We summarily fired our first scary accountant and didn't look back for years.

13

The Bubble Catches Fire

1996

BackRub, Google's precursor, comes online

9,272 organizations find themselves unlisted after the InterNIC drops their name service as a result of not having paid their domain name fee

Domain name tv.com sold to CNET for US$15,000

The Internet Ad Hoc Committee announces plans to add 7 new generic Top Level Domains (gTLD): .firm, .store, .web, .arts, .rec, .info, .nom. The IAHC plan also calls for a competing group of domain registrars worldwide.

A malicious cancelbot is released on USENET wiping out more than 25,000 messages

The WWW browser war, fought primarily between Netscape and Microsoft, has rushed in a new age in software development, whereby new releases are made quarterly with the help of Internet users eager to test upcoming (beta) versions. Internet2 project is kicked off by representatives from 34 universities on 1 Oct (:msb:)

China: requires users and ISPs to register with the police

Germany: cuts off access to some newsgroups carried on CompuServe

Saudi Arabia: confines Internet access to universities and hospitals

Singapore: requires political and religious content providers to register with the state

New Zealand: classifies computer disks as "publications" that can be censored and seized

source: Human Rights Watch

Technologies of the Year: Search engines, JAVA, Internet Phone

Emerging Technologies: Virtual environments (VRML)

[HOBBES' INTERNET TIMELINE]

For a while as the pressure built, as what was possible became ever more exciting. I existed in a double world, of both web sites and domain names. We were literally inventing the internet in real time. Not the internet of technology, not the internet of clever computer coding and technological products, but the internet of content. We were the entrepreneurs of what people would find online and we added huge value to the operatives, the investors and the financiers who were now flocking into the space.

Our original offices in the basement of Cyberia gave us a worm's eye view of those first heady days of progress. Although we were hidden downstairs, we used the café as our works canteen and spent hours there. It was a perfect meeting place for potential clients and we'd often find that someone we wanted to talk to was keen to visit anyway. We could give them a behind the scenes visit and introduction which added to our prestige. The space was also used for endless product launches and demonstrations and for a while we found that we were a ending one of these in almost every night of the week before heading out to the pubs and clubs of Soho. Indeed, it truly was suddenly a glorious time to be alive and we found ourselves at the centre of a crazy world of internet ideas and businesses. Every chancer in the country who wanted to jump on the bandwagon made their way to our door. This must be what Carnaby Street was like in the heyday of the Beatles, I thought in an idle moment, emerging from yet another event in the upstairs world.

Not only did we have the Internet café, Cyberia, above us, but above them a fast-growing ISP, Easynet, perched at the top of the building. Each of us were inventing and reinventing our worlds at the same time. To complete the maelstrom (and, eventually, to force us out), our landlords let out the other half of our space. They had built us a wall with windows across the basement and we had become used to having a protective shell around our fast-expanding world, but a new tenant moved in, an outfit invented and run by a television entrepreneur called Lenny Barshack. The space was named Sub-Cyberia and became an event and partying room plugged in to the upstairs world and the wider world of new age techno hippies. Lenny was incredibly friendly. He had the space painted in glorious colours and brought in a vintage hand operated Gaggia espresso machine. We welcomed our new neighbour and soon learnt to operate the coffee press, making ourselves endless high strength espressos to power us through our increasingly mad workload.

The downside of this new arrangement soon became apparent: Sub-Cyberia threw evening parties while we tried to work late into the night. Not only was it hard to resist joining in when there was free booze and interesting punters and loud music in the space next door, but if we ignored them they would not ignore us and would peer through the windows, gesticulating furiously.

The apotheosis of this came when upstairs Cyberia and downstairs Sub-Cyberia both ended up with contracts to host cable TV broadcasts — on the same night every week. The road outside would fill with television lorries and the stairs with huge cables as our world was invaded and broadcast in a way that didn't really fit with our worldview. It was time to move on.

Someone found us a large and cheap property a bit further West and we took out a lease. It was a collection of ratty old offices above some garages in a mews behind Baker Street. Steve and I went along to have a look and immediately loved the huge space. It had a hall type office with a warren of smaller spaces leading off it. We took it and signed a monthly lease which we could barely afford. When we came back on the following Monday morning half the ceiling had collapsed.

It turned out to be part of the last remaining Georgian block on Baker Street, owned by a notorious developer who had been trying for many years to get planning permission to knock the whole thing down. We had found a space that was big enough for us to expand in and expand was what we now needed to do. We set about filling the seemingly vast space with young designers, coders and salespeople.

For the first few weeks, after we moved our paltry belongings to our new home, we arrayed ourselves around the outside of the big space. We were still using doors placed on supports but now we were buying the door blanks from the hardware store. There were now five of us. In a sign of eventual separation, Mike the designer took an upstairs room where he could work in peace.

We immediately set out to hire more staff as we were starting to gain bigger contracts. I had suggested a project manager, and we found a woman from the newspaper industry, Liz, who was a godsend in the coming years. We advertised for a designer of our own and a fresh-faced boy arrived with his portfolio on a CD. I was so impressed with this piece of technical genius that I offered him a job on the spot. Gideon was fresh out of college and later confessed that his mum had told him to take the CD, but he was a brilliant hire. These core hires gave us more confidence and we pulled in some more projects and more staff. Within a few months the space that had seemed big enough to ride a bicycle around (one of my suggestions) was starting to seem rather cramped, but filled with energy, music and cigarette smoke as we grabbed hold of this new industry with both hands. We knew we were inventing something from scratch. Others were doing the same, of course, and we soon started to encounter other people who talked the same language.

We were meeting a lot of businesspeople. It was exciting, we really could see that we had something they didn't. However, I started to feel that I didn't quite connect with them. I decided it was because I was wearing my normal shoddy clothes. I went out and bought a suit at Jaeger. To me it was quite an investment and I loved it. I started wearing it and from that point on I wore suits every working day for the next five years.

By 1995 Microsoft was the dominant tech firm but their wealth and power came from the desktop operating system, Windows and, although Bill Gates talked about an internet strategy, it was clear to most observers that he had little interest in the space. There was comparatively little money in online tools compared to the vast wealth Microsoft accrued from its monopoly position on the desktop.

Microsoft came to London to launch the latest consumer iteration of their flagship product, Microsoft Network, a subscription-based dial-up online service and content provider which for a few short months convinced everyone that it would sweep away the Internet, and we all went along eagerly to see this mythical billionaire who had been the focus of much of our ire for years. He sat on the stage, a tiny figure, and I found a fantasy of someone getting up and shooting him wouldn't leave my head. Later, when I told a colleague about this, he told me he had the same thoughts. Gates had descended like an alien into our little world, showing us that we were not alone nor unthreatened by much bigger fish.

The Microsoft Network was presented through an artificial folder-like graphical user interface integrated into the Windows Explorer file management program, with a home page named

'MSN Central'. Categories on MSN appeared like folders in the file system. It was included with Windows 95 installations and promoted through Windows and other Microsoft software released at the time. Product support and discussion was offered through the MSN service, as well as information such as news and weather, basic email capabilities, chat rooms, and message boards similar to newsgroups. It also offered access to the Internet via Internet Explorer.

There was debate in the media as to whether MSN would be an 'Internet killer', and some companies hedged their bets for the first year, creating content both on MSN and the World Wide Web. However, MSN launched too late to be a real threat to the web.

Microsoft launched MSN at the very cusp of the consumer Internet. We finally had a couple of graphical web browsers (Netscape, Mosaic). Internet Explorer (which started as Mosaic), however, was not even part of the initial Windows 95 release. It showed up later. Awareness and demand for Internet access were growing at precisely the moment that millions of people were bringing computers into their home for the very first time. When they used these browsers and, often, AOL to access the Internet, it was mostly through Windows 95. In the end, humanity's first experiences with the World Wide Web would be forever tied to Microsoft's platform and, later, Internet Explorer (though that's a tale for another time). Following Bill Gates' internal 'Internet Tidal Wave memo', which refocused Microsoft to be Internet-centric, MSN began to move its content to the web and promote itself more actively as an Internet service provider.

It also didn't take long for ad agencies to notice what we were doing and we started to get attention from them. A guy called Rob Norman from CIA came sniffing around Webmedia. He told us he wanted to do a great deal, that he would buy Webmedia and move us into the CIA offices as part of his global growth policy. He invited us to visit their premises and took us on a tour. At one point he opened a door and revealed a team of people who looked like they were trapped at the end of a corridor. Steve and I later worked out that they were another company that he had previously absorbed, and that would be our fate if we allowed ourselves to be bought.

To be honest, it was far too early to be selling out and we were having too much fun, but it gave us some ideas about where we were headed. By the end of 1996 after a mad year of inventing the web business, learning to sell to clients, hire staff and make actual web sites, we had ended up with a decent roster of clients.

After we'd moved to the Baker Street mews and started getting real contracts from big customers our staff count rose dramatically. My idea of building an organisation to create web sites by dividing up the work and management was becoming a reality. Unfortunately, the complexity of the process was outstripping our ability to control the work. Nobody in the office had ever been through this before. In fact, nobody in the world had been through this before. It wasn't a matter of going out and hiring experienced executives or trained managers of the process — everybody was working from scratch and we were neither capitalised enough or experienced enough in our own right to keep control of the situation.

The only person knew who knew how internet protocols worked, who was a genuine nerd, was a guy called Steve Hebditch. I had met him when I was working with Time Out to start their web presence. He was already on the scene, sorting various computer things out. I soon got him involved with our first few projects at Webmedia and he became an important part of the team, although never an employee. He had an independent streak but he could deliver and made us seem at least a bit credible.

Another person I knew from the arcane world of computer programming was our Loophole Cinema sound person, Ben Hayman. I was chatting to him one day and he told me that his actual daytime job was building information systems for banks in 4G languages. This didn't mean anything to me. I knew that banks had nothing to teach us in terms of the internet or building web sites, but my ears did prick up when he said information systems.

I had been thinking about how we were going to manage all the parts of the web sites we were building. I realised that Ben's basic skill was understanding how to manage all the moving parts and that he was almost certainly good at this, but he didn't know anything about the internet, about internet protocols and web servers and h p and all the things that were starting to dominate our lives. There were no tools for this but, in a little epiphany I realised that if I could put internet protocols and information systems together, we might have something really useful.

In 1996 I got Ben and Steve together and told them my thinking. It must have made sense because they started working on a project that was initially called Webservices, another spin out from the Webmedia project. We gave them desk space in our new Baker Street offices and they gave us a seat on their board. For a while I was a director of this company which, without me realising it, was inventing a new thing called a CMS or Computer Management System.

> *Webdevelopment Ltd. is a young, creative Internet software development company, building intelligent business applications that use the Web to support information publishing, collaborative working, or rapid business change.*
>
> *The use of the latest development languages and techniques allow the development of secure, platform independent applications that can take advantage of existing desktop hardware.*
>
> *Having secured venture funding from investment capital group 3i, the company has extended its development and services capabilities, with a strong sales and marketing drive, and is currently expanding its program of industry partnerships.*
>
> **WEBDEVELOPMENT WEBSITE IN 1997**

By the middle of 1998 they had secured the first of many venture capital fundings from 3i and were expanding fast. They had moved into a bunch of offices connected to ours and brought more people into the mix. Early in 1999 they changed their name to Mediasurface and escaped the orbit of Webmedia, but by that time I was also gone from the Webmedia world with my own baby startup, NetNames.

At Internet World in London in 1995 we met a young Malaysian man who was interested in what we were doing. Sensing some business opportunity, and wanting to see some more of the world, I decided I really had to fly out to visit him. Money had begun to flow through our bank account and, although our bank manager hated us, we were starting to feel confident in the company.

I flew out to Kuala Lumpur to a wall of sweltering heat and afternoon rainstorms. Richard took me out to eat at local restaurants and explained his small but busy ad agency to me. Unfortunately, it was a world that I had little interest in, but he was well connected and introduced me all around town. After I got home he gave us a small amount of work, part of which involved registering domain names for his project in Hong Kong and Malaysia and the upshot of this was my next epiphany.

Domain names at this time were a wild west. We knew how to register .com domains and our local .uk versions, both of which required little more than access to email. There were no proper registries and it was unclear who was in control of most domains. Although registrations were on the whole free, it was a complicated business and most people didn't bother or let their Internet service provider do a domain registration. In the US a tiny company called Network Solutions had the contract to manage .com,

.net and .org, but as the number of domain name registrations grew faster and faster, greedy eyes started to eye the contract.

Anyway, nobody much was looking at this space and nobody thought much of it, but after I finished a job for Richard which included registering a domain name for him in Hong Kong and Malaysia, I felt rather pleased with myself. It had been a lot of work to find out how to do the registrations, but I idly mused that if anyone ever asked me again to do registrations in those countries, it would be easy. This speculation suddenly hit me like a speeding train. Rather than wonder if anyone would ever ask me again, I thought, why not offer to do the registrations. And if these countries were possible, what was going on in all the other countries of the world.

I asked Steve if I could spend a bit of money on research and when he agreed I put out an advert for someone to do a small research project. I wanted someone to look at a lot of countries around the world and find out how to register domain names in them. A short while later a student called Mark Henderson-Thynne got in touch. He'd already done a large part of the research for me and offered it as proof of his ability to get paid to do the rest. I was fairly impressed and I gave him the contract. After I'd met him and looked at what he had come up with I asked him if he would like to come to work with us and help start a domain name registration service. Although he was as student he happily dropped out of college and came to work in the Webmedia offices. He was the first employee of my new venture and we moved our desks to the corner of the big office and started work.

When I first thought up NetNames I didn't think of it as a major initiative but just as an interesting add on service for Web-media. I had realised that registering domain names was sometimes a tricky business and I was intrigued by how it was done around the world. More than that, I had noticed that lots of businesses were using the email and web addresses that their service provides gave them. Not only were these ugly, but they had no long-term stability. Why would you use a business address that contained someone else's name? I thought there was an opportunity to help companies to own their own names, but I didn't really think through all the ramifications of that service.

After we had set up a rudimentary system for managing registration orders and had hired a third member of the NetNames team, Catherine, I wondered how we could advertise such a strange new service. In those days when most information had not yet percolated online, newspapers like The Times would list the entire stock market with prices every day, using up entire pages to do so. I asked Mark to run a quick check on part of the listings, to see how many firms seemed to have registered a domain name. He came back after a bit of work and told me that it seemed that very few had. 'Below ten percent, I'd say'. The stock market listings always had one advertisement in a box in the centre of the page. Taking Mark's view of how few had their own names, I came up with an advert that said, 'Fewer than 10% of these companies have protected their name for use on the Internet', with arrows pointing out to the company names that would surround it. We managed to buy a placing on that page and the advert ran. It was a huge success and years later I would tell people that we only really advertised once, after which the phones never stopped ringing and the business took on a life of its own. To be honest, we did try to book the same slot again but never managed to get hold of it as it was highly sought after. Never mind, it did a lot more than we thought it would and we were off.

The idea of owning a domain name was new to companies but the idea of internet business was just starting to take off and it soon became clear that we had found a great new business niche. Over the next few months our team grew, we moved to side offices and our turnover increased rapidly. More than that, we became the go to company for domain names and for domain name stories in the press just as Webmedia started to suffer from being in a newly highly competitive market. I had no idea of the domain name wars to come nor of the implosion of Webmedia, but I was up and running again. I let Steve take on day-to-day responsibility for the web side of the business while focused on my new creation.

After we moved to our new offices we installed a 30-line ISDN cabinet and a proper internet leased line. For the first time we were independent and in control of all our own services. Out in the world people were still using dial up on their home lines. Wi-Fi was unknown, everything had to be plugged in to Ethernet cables. Even our computers didn't tend to come with networking built in, but we were learning fast and creating a version of the new world. Business continued to grow and the phone lines were busy. We started to ramp up our staff numbers and our business soared as we signed up some major customers. Then one morning we found that we had no phone lines at all and thus no connection to the outside world. We contacted British Telecom, our suppliers, and they promised to investigate. We plugged a single phone into the fax line, which was still working, and waited to resume business. The office quickly filled with smoke as the designers and salespeople sat around doing nothing.

This situation went on for the next few days and started to drive us insane. Nobody could contact us and our customers were starting to think we had gone bust. British Telecom sent an engineer who examined our setup an told us it was our switchboard that wasn't working. The switchboard people came and told us it was certainly the phone lines. After we had been around this circuit a few times I felt I was going mad and I came up with a plan. I registered a domain name, britishtelecom.com and put up a web site that complained about the situation and about British Telecom in general. I asked our key designer, Gideon, for a logo and he quickly made me an intertwined pair of red and blue steaming turds, based on the then current BT logo of pan who was split into red and blue, both listening and speaking.

We made the web site live and I called a couple of people knew in the press, who wrote about it. Within a few hours I had a senior BT executive in the office, solicitously assuring me that they would solve the problem and swiftly some real engineers arrived and tracked down the issues. Once the phones were fixed and BT had agreed to pay us compensation for the disaster they had caused, they asked me to take the website down. By now it had become quite popular and we'd taken to listing a lot of other problems people had with their telecoms, so I refused. 'That wasn't part of the deal,' I said, and it hadn't been, but the corporation didn't take this very kindly. A few weeks later a fat writ landed on my desk, claiming that they owned the copyright on britishtelecom.com and asking the court to take the site down and return their property to them. I didn't think this was true so I set out to find a decent lawyer and fight the case.

I'm not sure now why I wanted so desperately to fight such a huge corporation, whose writ ended with the ominous point that they were a plc who had profits of six hundred million pounds in the most recent year. The site we had put up using the domain name had attracted quite a lot of attention and I was proud of it. I suppose it was giving me some good marketing, but that wasn't really the point. I just felt that British Telecom shouldn't be able to grab back a domain just because they wanted it. If I was smart enough to realise they should register their own names, then they should be too. It was the first domain name case of its kind and I went out to find a decent lawyer who could build a defence. I did this and we spent a few months to and froing with the BT lawyers. Then my lawyer, who seemed to be hugely enjoying himself, asked me if I could afford the case. 'Of course I can,' I said. 'You'll probably need about a hundred thousand pounds if it goes to trial. You ok with that?'

I wasn't, of course. I didn't really have any spare cash, and nor did NetNames or Webmedia. I realised I needed a way out. I let it ride for a few more weeks, then I suggested we sound them out for a settlement. They were more than happy to settle and after a bit more haggling (they wanted me to agree never to register anything with the letters 'bt' in it) we came to an agreement. I came away with a small but decent settlement with which I bought a foot launched paraglider, a sport that I was keen to take up.

By now we had a range of clients, though most of them seemed to be banks, building societies and airlines. We had launched a site for the Cheltenham and Gloucester building society and one for Time Out, my old employer who had come along for the ride. In August we discussed what other opportunities were available and decided to start a publishing arm which we called Webcontent. We hired Sam Michel who had also been at Time Out and brought him in to work on this new project.

Sam had done some work with student unions and he suggested starting a comedy website. After a few months' work we launched ComedyWeb, MovieWeb and StudentWeb. We thought we could sell advertising on them. We also spent a lot of time trying to get the right to publish television listings so we could start a TV web site. We knew that this sort of content was coming and we wanted to be in at the start, but we didn't really have the resources or experience to pull it off. By the end of the year the experiment was over, having distracted us from the web agency business and absorbed a lot of our cashflow.

In the outside world, new internet publications were multiplying — and I was writing for many of them. A publisher at Emap, Roger Green, had started a magazine called Internet and I had a column in it. I discussed starting some content sites with Emap, assuming they would have a lot more resources to invest. I had registered a domain name called Whatsnew.com and proposed giving it to them for a share in a new site about new things on the internet. As What's New sites were one of the most popular destinations at the time they were interested but the project fizzled soon after starting. Getting the content side of the web equation right was going to be harder than it looked.

In December 1996 the UK version of Wired, just about the hippest magazine in the world at the time, put Steve and I on the cover of what turned out to be their penultimate UK copy. I had been to the launch party for the UK version of Wired at a nightclub in Holborn where the founders, Louis Rossetto and Jane Metcalfe, were held away from the likes of us by a ring of steel. They handed out badges saying Get Wired. Douglas Rushkoff said, "In a sense, Wired UK never really existed. It was an American publication with a particular agenda masquerading as a British effort. No doubt they will continue to distribute their ideas throughout England, but at least they'll be doing so a bit more honestly: They'll simply export the US edition of Wired, which is all they really meant to do in the first place." The cover image had a bunch of hip young technorati jumping in the air. The combination of Steve and myself made us look ridiculous. However, it was a Wired cover and wasn't to be argued with. Also, it had the words, 'Write Code. Have Fun. Make Money.' We couldn't write code but we liked being cover stars.

We had a full-page advert in the same issue, marking our second anniversary and claiming 80 years of web experience. I can't remember if we bought it because we were in the issue or whether they gave it to us for some reason, but there it is in all its Technicolor glory. I suggested a birthday cake for the ad but our designers used an ugly baby. Which Online, one of our projects, also took a third page advert and there is even a long letter from one of our staff, Chris Thorpe in the mag.

At the time we looked dominant, like the magazine itself, but dark clouds were gathering unseen.

I finally moved out of Hackney, to Camden, into a lovely rented flat right behind the high street. We'd had enough of Hackney and wanted something slightly more elegant. By chance we found something quite stupendous.

My partner was working as a lawyer nearby and had found the flat. The flat was hidden away behind a row of alms houses on Bayham Street, St Martins Almshouses, and was the ground floor of a Georgian house. It sat alongside another house and a chapel. Behind this row of houses was a park, converted from the grave-yard of this place. There were even leftover graves in our back gar-den. The place was wonderful, so hidden away from the noise and dust of Camden, yet right there in the centre of London. It had belonged to a Shakespearean actress of note, Brenda Bruce, who had recently died and left it to her two daughters. As it had some subsidence issues, they had decided to let it out while they sorted out the underpinning, and we had stumbled on it at the right moment.

There seemed to be more Internet World shows than ever and we tried to get to most of them, both in London, the rest of the UK and in the US on the East and West coasts. They were a combina-tion of a jolly and business trip, never less than fun. These shows got huge fast. The early little shows became distant memories. Of the three 'Meckler maidens' that I had met at the first event in London, one, Pam, stayed working for Alan Meckler and became the floor manager for the biggest show of all, the Los Angeles Internet World. Another, Tarnya, was working for us at Webmedia and the third, Jackie, had set up her own PR company, Flapjack, and did all my PR for years. It was like we'd all grown into the industry and it into us.

In London the shows soon transferred to the biggest venues. The New York show occupied the Jacob Javits centre, a vast eighties monstrosity that was reputedly owned and controlled by the mafia. The West Coast show moved after a couple of years from San Jose to Los Angeles, into a vast new exhibition space on the edge of town. Our season started to revolve around New York and Los Angeles where we would hang out, drink madly, pick up on industry gossip and try to keep up with the mad, infinite helter-skelter world of the Internet.

I'd started my international expansion by opening a New York office. I managed to expand by asking around for a partner in the US. One of our managers at Webmedia, a dual national American Brit called Elizabeth told me she had a brother, Anthony, who was working on something to do with the internet in New York. He sounded interesting so I flew out to meet him and discuss starting an office.

Anthony and his sister were smart academic types who hadn't quite made it into academia. Their parents were paleologists and Tony had been born in Kenya when it was still called Rhodesia.

He had dabbled in arts related projects over the years but at that point was trying to get an online business started. He had an office in the meat packing district on West 14th Street, an area of New York that was at that time still very rough and ready — just my sort of place. While the office was rather nice, downstairs they still literally packed meat. Huge lorries would arrive from all over the US and they would back up and unload endless carcasses of beef and other animals. I never quite found out what was going on downstairs, but sometimes in the summer you would encounter a huge single kidney or a side of bones sitting on the sidewalk.

That part of town was fun though. Around the corner was a legendary biker's bar called Hogs and Heifers which we never went into but which we knew had hundreds of bras hanging over the bar. It was a bit intimidating but it added to the local colour. There were some pretty good bistros on the block and you could walk to the Hudson in a few minutes. It wasn't the nicest part of town. At night it was a transvestite hooker cruising zone. Anthony told me a story of trying to mend a flat tyre one night and hearing a voice asking if he needed help. He looked up from under his car to see a huge woman with rippling muscles offering to help.

Through the area ran an abandoned train line that later became the Highline. The elevated road that had previously run down the west side of Manhattan had recently been removed and the whole area was, in retrospect, being lined up for gentrification. But in the 90s it was rough - and cheap.

Anthony and his friends were working on a project for the American sex education council, which turned out to be a private company offering what was mostly legalised porn. We discussed NetNames at length and he was keen to join in and start the US version. He asked me if I wanted to continue to develop the porn site, suggesting that Webmedia would be a good partner for this, but I had to tell him there was no way I would ever consider it. The idea horrified me. A while before Steve had handled and enquiry from a company in London called Northern and Shell, a publisher of pornographic magazines run by the man who later acquired the Express newspaper group. We had had to come up with a 'no dubious projects' rule on the spot and I was determined to stick to it.

On the other hand, Tony turned out to be a good partner, for a few years at least. We did a deal that gave him part ownership of NetNames USA and he quickly got the office up and running. I made him a lot of promises of support and shared technology developments and, although I tried to make it all happen, I found that I could never quite come up with what he wanted.

Within a few months I had a base and a thriving business in the US, which gave me more clout in the fast-developing industry and a good reason to visit regularly.

14

Megalomedia

1997

The American Registry for Internet Numbers (ARIN)is established to handle administration and registration of IP numbers to the geographical areas currently handled by Network

In protest of the DNS monopoly, AlterNIC's owner, Eugene Kashpureff, hacks DNS so users going to www.internic.net end up at www.alternic.net

Domain name business.com sold for US$150,000

Early in the morning of 17 July, human error at Network Solutions causes the DNS table for .com and .net domains to become corrupted, making millions of systems unreachable.

Longest hostname registered with InterNIC: CHALLENGER.MED.SYNAPSE.UAH.UALBERTA.CA

101,803 Name Servers in whois database

RFC 2100: The Naming of Hosts

Technologies of the Year: Push, Multicasting

Emerging Technologies: Push

[HOBBES' INTERNET TIMELINE]

A couple of smart kids at university in the US registered a domain name for their startup and Google was born, though nobody knew it. A new era had arrived though we had no idea how it would change our lives. Up to then we had been using various fairly useless search engines such as Alta Vista and Excite. By the beginning of 1999 the founders of Google tried to sell their startup to an existing search engine, Excite, for $750,000, but the CEO turned them down in possibly the worst business decision since someone failed to sign the Beatles. At this point I was worth more than Google, though that didn't last long.

The Internet was really coming to life and turning into a huge financial game across the world and, although I didn't know it at the time, the game was coming to an end for me. The early days of the Internet, the wild west, the anything goes time, the everything has to be invented, the period when there were only two men and a dog online and nobody knew the dog was a dog — these days were about to end in the most dramatic way. Of course, I didn't know that or care about it. Everything seemed more exciting than it could possibly be and I was still strapped in for the ride. For the first time in my life, I was earning a decent amount of money. One thing Neil had done at Webmedia was to push Steve and my salaries up to a decent level. He also suggested we get company cars and I soon found myself with a funky open topped Saab, the best car I'd ever had.

With my partner we decided we had to leave grimy Hackney for somewhere a bit more salubrious. She was working in Camden and found us a wonderful flat just off the main road, behind the alms houses that lined the street. The flat had belonged to an actress, Brenda Bruce, who had recently died and left it to her daughters. We fell into a new life, close to Regents Park. We weren't rich and our life remained much the same, but things were looking up. We left Hackney and settled into Camden. Soon our first child was on the way.

In 1996 the domain name tv.com sold to Cnet for $15,000. This seemed like a watershed in pricing, but by the next year Business.com was sold for $150,000. Dozens of country domains were registered for the first time, many of them by us, including Libya (.ly), Turkmenistan (.tm) and Tuvalu (.tv). We had noticed that many of these domains were simply not in the registry and also that the process for putting one in was beyond simple: you had to find a national of that country and submit a request to IANA in their name with yourself as the registry. We started to do this in earnest because we also recognised the earning potential of domains such as .tm and .tv. In fact, others already had their eyes on .tv for obvious use as a television domain. With retrospect this was an outrageous colonialist attitude to these places, wanting to use their entire country level domains for our own greedy purposes. But all the same, the domain world was still a wild west and we were mired deep within it.

Early in 1997 I was standing in the NetNames office when the phone rang. It rings a lot and there were other people about to answer it but as I was on my own for a moment I picked it up. It was my partner. 'I'm pregnant,' she said.

It was not unexpected. We had always wanted children since we first got together. Our running joke was that we would have tousle haired children because both of our hair is so curly. And I always loved babies, always assumed I would have them, never had any doubt. It was a major moment and I was very happy, my family had started, but there were nine months to go and life had to go on. I didn't think too much about what might change. The business was doing reasonably well, we were living in a wonderful flat with a garden and both working at things we enjoy. Life was looking good.

Webmedia was growing fast as a high tide started to lift all boats. We had had an advantage at first, but now had a fair amount of other startups and established advertising agencies were getting into our marketplace. We went looking for someone to help us raise some money to expand. We didn't really understand how to raise money or what we would use it for. I don't recall any planning or plan, which was going to become a feature of my companies and possibly their biggest weakness.

The only cloud on the horizon was the seeming stagnation of Webmedia. I had drawn back from hands on management of Webmedia. NetNames was now my baby with huge potential whereas Webmedia had become a bit of a problem child having grown so fast. We had a good team, but things are not so easy to manage. We had to invent everything from scratch, there were no off the shelf tools to make life easy. Our young and headstrong team smoked in the office, played music all the time (we even had DJ decks in the office) and went out partying nonstop. There was more competition every day, from big agencies and nimble start-ups. They all have more management experience than us. Let's face it, we had no management experience.

We had no team, no board, no nothing. Webmedia needed help and I wasn't really the person to bring it. My attention deficit was playing out as usual and I'd lost a lot of interest in the Webb game. NetNames, on the other hand, was exactly at the state I liked my projects to be — in the early stages of life. It was new enough to be interesting and had little competition. That will come later, of course, but for the time being our revenues were growing fast. I suspected that we were subsidising Webmedia, keeping it afloat, and that thought ate me up at night. I wanted to do something about it but I wasn't sure what.

Steve and I hired a finance guru. He had recently been made redundant from Merrill Lynch. Neil Black was a small guy who didn't lack in confidence. He drove a new TVR which had a number plate with P64 in it, the name of the redundancy tax form. He had bought it with his Merrill Lynch payoff and, although we couldn't really all fit into it, he took us out for a spin in the rain, telling us he'd been warned not to go anywhere when it was wet because the car would break down. It was like a metaphor for my relationship with him.

We tasked him with finding us investment money and in return we gave him some shares in the company, dependent on success. While he set about his mission he had other impacts on the company. He asked how much Steve and I were earning from our company and then insisted that we hugely ramp up our salaries.

After that I was earning more than I would ever earn again. He also suggested that we should have company cars. We didn't want to fail him and we rather liked his suggestions so Steve and I both went about ordering reasonably fancy cars. He went out looking for an investor, and it didn't take long before he hit paydirt.

By August he persuaded a company run by the Saatchi's CEO to take a stake in Webmedia. The company, Megalomedia, had been set up with investment from the advertising brothers to build a portfolio of holdings in media companies. Megalomedia was run by a man called Christopher Parker who had been the finance director of Saatchi and Saatchi in their glory days. They had invested in a couple of semi-technology companies and when Neil came knocking they seemed keen to make an investment in us. Steve and I practised saying how much our company was worth without laughing. It was hard to say figures in the millions. We had a feeling that we were arriving, and the investors seemed excellent, but I was nervous. 'I got the wrong Saatchi,' I told people afterwards, mindful that Charles Saatchi had been the spectre at my art degree.

I didn't really have much to do with the negotiations of the deal. Neil had been incentivised with share options to make it happen and he was determined to earn his slice. While I was on holiday in France that year I got a call, 'Come back now and sign the deal.' I left my family in France and jumped on a plane. Soon we had half a million quid in the bank and a couple of new directors on the board. Things would never be the same again.

I was pleased to get proper investors as my first child was coming close to its due date and I wanted to feel secure in the world. Soon after the deal closed we got invited to a meal at the Ivy to dine with our new overlords. It was a touch of glamour, but we didn't know what would happen next. I assumed it would be big.

The new arrangements didn't last very long. Megalomedia brought on board two new directors from one of their other investments, Framestore. The husband-and-wife team soon realised that we were a bit of a joke outfit without much idea of where we were going and they started to turn the thumbscrews. I never got on very well with them and in addition, our finance saviour, Neil, went on being Neil. It soon occurred to me that he was trying to manipulate us into a situation where the investors would buy out the rest of the shareholders. The reason for this was obvious: he now owned a chunk of our stock but it would only become valuable if he could sell it.

An attempt to manipulate the relationship between Steve and me and the other directors led to a breakdown between me and the rest. Steve, sensibly, stayed on board, but I got cross with the whole situation and started to feel I needed a way out. Of course, I had NetNames which I thought was subsidising the whole business and which certainly had a lot of potential. I knew that NetNames was a good business and it went on growing in the corner of Webmedia. I didn't yet really understand the scope of it, how it was going to revolve around intellectual property or how fast the internet was going to grow, but I could see it was working. I decided I didn't really care what happened with Webmedia so long as I kept my baby. When relationships with Megalomedia reached rock bottom I made a suggestion. They could keep the whole Webmedia business if I could take NetNames in return. The offer was too tempting for them to turn down and, although I suspected they knew it was really a bad deal, the split went ahead. This time it was done by real lawyers and accountants and took a few months to push through, but by August that year I was freed, our split became official.

My time as a Web entrepreneur was over. The company I had started with Steve barely three years earlier and which had grown to be a leading web company, was no longer my company. I took some investment from Keith Teare and moved to a floor above a bed shop on Tottenham Court Road with my loyal staff. The domain name wars were up and running and it suddenly seemed like the most exciting space in the world.

Eighteen years of Tory rule was also coming to an end and this time, this time we were sure Labour would come good. None of us wanted a repeat of that dreadful night when we'd sat up to welcome a new Labour government only to find the ridiculous John Major romped home, destroying the life and career of the Welsh windbag, Neil Kinnock. Blair was different, he was young and modern. He lived in Islington, of course, when Islington was still somewhere to aspire to.

I went to Geneva, to the World Trade Organisation, and sat for a couple of days in their huge auditoriums while we discussed the future of domain names with simultaneous translation into all European languages. In some ways it was dull but in others it was deadly exciting because my baby was now reaching into the highest echelons of international power. I felt I had an opportunity to ride with the subject to the very top but I was also aware that the dangers of being side-lined existed. I wasn't a normal bureaucrat; I didn't represent one of the big players and I had my own very specific vested interests — I wanted the best for Net-Names. I wasn't scared to be irksome and to speak up, not good characteristics in those sorts of environments. I must have been vaguely aware that the domain name wars were breaking out, but in the calm cloistered world of Geneva that all seemed a long way away. I was growing used to the inner sanctums of the world order, simultaneous translation, more and more official government delegates muscling in on my territory. I was alone as always and stayed in a small hotel in the town.

My last day there, May 1st, was the day of the UK general election but I was too busy to pay much attention to the final hours of the campaign. I went to a pub near my hotel where they were showing the results but, after a couple of beers I realised again that it wasn't much fun staying up for election night all alone and I went back to my hotel. I slept all night with the television on, waking fitfully to see strange results announced. The drama mingled with my dreams and to this day when people ask the standard question, were you up for Portillo I can't answer, not knowing whether I woke and saw the announcement or dreamed it intermingled with all the other drama.

In the morning I had an early flight into London airport and sunshine. Everybody had a fixed grin on their faces, nobody could stop smiling, grinning from ear to ear. I talked to my taxi driver at length and he was of course a fervent Labour supporter, everyone suddenly was, a great new era had dawned and we were all happy and modern and going to be wealthy, or at least not poor. In my heart I knew that this was not a left-wing country and that the huge victory would not end well, but on that morning it seemed possible that we were truly born anew.

I gathered a few friends and took them for a celebratory meal at the Atlantic, that great glorious subterranean 90s restaurant in the bowels of a hotel that was for a short period almost our office canteen. We ate and drank and laughed and I paid the huge bill, then staggered off to Carnaby Street where we drank Pimms although we were well past needing any drink. Something huge had changed, the world had turned and I was excited about what came next.

My son was born on October 14, 1997, at UCL, a huge hospital that happened to be situated right behind my office on Tottenham Court Road. He was born in the early morning and by the time the world was awake I was in my office emailing photos of him to my family. It so happened that the same day was the deadline for sending an application to join the new domain name organisation, CORE. I had to get my documents notarised, something that we never did in London. I located a notary across London and set out with the documents, leaving mother and new-born in the maternity ward. It seemed to take hours to get the documents first signed off and then entrusted to a courier for overnight delivery to New York. The moment that was done I seemed to emerge from a bubble back into the real world. I was wearing a T-shirt; it was raining and I realised I hadn't eaten all day. More, I had a new baby to return to. I mentally dumped the domain name industry and returned to my short parental leave.

15

Webmedia 1994-1998

Webmedia suddenly went bust at the end of 1997. It came unexpectedly to me. I had stopped paying any attention to it and was busy and focused on NetNames. I didn't mind falling out with the people now in control of the company, but I was unhappy about falling out with Steve. Webmedia was my baby, my first venture into real internet services and it was a tragedy to see it go. To this day I still have no idea why a big operator like Saatchi's Megalomedia could just dump an innovator like that. The losses were small and the upside, as was about to be revealed, was gigantic. Webmedia has invented a new thing, had carved out a service that hadn't existed before we came along. Steve and I weren't the best managers in the world, but we'd acknowledged that by bringing in a supposedly professional team. But no, rather than boost the company or reinvent it, the investors had shut it down.

Web production company Webmedia has gone into voluntary liquidation, with 17 redundancies. Webmedia Group, the holding company, said it would continue to provide strategic advice to new media clients, but was pulling out of the production market. It is retaining just three staff, although chairman and chief executive Steve Bowbrick claimed it wanted to recruit more.[9]

It seemed like a lifetime since we'd been in Soho, hanging out in The Living Room and willing ourselves to invent a new type of company — but it was only just over three years. The company had lasted from 1994 and had barely staggered into 1998. To most people in the world the internet was still a mystery, a fad or a waste of time, and most companies were still doing nothing in the space. None of the modern services that we have come to rely on existed. The thing had barely got out of the starting blocks, yet Steve and I had not only started a company and built a multi-million-pound turnover, but we'd managed to go bust before most people had come to the table. A failed company isn't usually a reason for boasting, but I've always had a place in my heart for that brief flowering of, if not a thousand flowers, certainly of a few hundred. Unfortunately, Mao's dictum came to its natural conclusion — we flowered early and had our heads lopped off for our temerity.

I was lucky, I had felt it coming and had been given an opportunity to escape. Steve not so, whatever fine words were bandied about at the time he was destined to spend the next few years in the dark depths, trying to fight his way out of the hole that Megalomedia and their crew had made for him.

By the start of 1998 the previously exciting list of client companies on their web site was replaced by a deathly holding statement:

The Internet has changed. The third wave of web sites, reaching deep into the way we do business, is now live. It's not a marketing medium, it's not a promotional tool, it's not even the Point of

Sale it's the site of a profound reinvention of the way we create, communicate and trade. Some of the most important businesses in Britain took their first steps onto the web with Webmedia (and their second and third...) and now we're taking them further - defining Internet business strategy and helping managers to adapt to the new, connected era.

It wasn't all bad. Our young team were released and spread out across the media landscape, taking the skills and attitude they had learnt at Webmedia to new heights. I was happy that most of them went to media companies such as The Guardian and the BBC rather than to agencies. The world of internet design and build companies was going to grow massively over the next few years but it was also going to become far blander and less entertaining than our few years at the helm had been. I have to admit I didn't pay much attention to how my first company fell apart or where people went, but I've kept in touch with most of them over the years and they are all pathfinders in the industry.

As for Steve, he entered a bleak period of his life, sequestered in a room in Soho pretending to be doing consultancy while his company was ignored and depleted by those who were supposed to take it to new heights. To this day I believe that they had no idea what the Web was going to bring and conflicting ambitions within the group laid low what should have been a defining agency of the .com years. Somehow they managed to destroy a pathfinder company and scatter a foundational crew to the four winds. Maybe it was the Saatchis once again proving they had little taste for innovation, maybe it was others, more concerned with their own worlds. Either way, Webmedia was destroyed just as the world opened up to our message: let a thousand flowers bloom.

Webmedia Ltd, 1994-1998

Oct 1994
Founded in small office beneath Cyberia internet cafe
Launches site for Time Out

April 1995
Bowbrick offers to sell a share of the company to an 'individual with loads of money'

June
BT sues over britishtelecom.com site which catalogues problems with Webmedia's
ISDN line. Case settled out of court

August
Backs launch of New Media Marketing and Sales
Megalomedia acquires 11% share for £200,000 cash with option to buy further 10%

October
Cheltenham & Gloucester switches Web site account to DNA Communications

November
Webcontent re-absorbed into main company.
Ivan Pope pushes NetNames and flags up the new 'full-service agency' business strategy
Net pioneer Bill Washburn joins as international Strategic adviser

Feb 1996

Three people made redundant in 'routine' cuts

March

The (Web) market is bull, bull, bull. Growth is still huge and structural.

There will be consolidation..." says Bowbrick.

Launches site for Youthnet

April

Revamp as an 'agency' offering value-added services over pure production.

'This shift is not an option,' says Bowbrick.

Business development manager, Tanya Norse, leaves Webmedia for Poppe Tyson

May

Launches site for Radio 4 after a year of wrangles. Cost £10,000

June

Appointed online strategy advisers to Friends of the Earth

August

Legal and General appoints Black Sun Interacive after pitch which includes Webmedia

Relaunches Lufthansa's site

Hired to re-build Nationwide's English Football League site

Co-founder Ivan Pope quits the Webmedia board in an amicable demerger to concentrate on NetNames.

Megalomedia increases its stake from 18.5% to 43%

September

Online strategy director, Sam Michel, sets up the UK Net Marketing discussion list,

sponsored by Webmedia.

Appoints two new account managers

Hired by Alliance and Leicester to re-launch site

Peter Beech joins as Managing Director, poached from Leo Burnett. Bowbrick becomes CEO and chairman.

Lesley Phillips and Howard Hogan appointed as business development manager and financial controller respectively.

Webmedia features on LWTs Wannnabe show. The show is about careers advice.

October

Revamp of Blackwell's Online Bookshop site

Staffing slashed from 30 to 20 following strategic review. Production, admin and sales staff go.

Music Network culled from Webmedia's portfolio with loss of nine staff. Mc Tony Martin claims a catalogue of broken promises and mismatched expectations from Webmedia.

Bowbrick says, 'It's not a downturn in the market'.

Bowbrick criticises media companies for paying lip service to Labour's idea of stakeholding.

November

Marketing manager Steve Masters joins VNU New Media following redundancy.

1998 Jan

Webmedia Ltd liquidated with 17 jobs lost. Webmedia Group to concentrate on strategic consultancy.

(c) 1988 New Media VNU

16

The Domain Name Wars

1998

Hobbes' Internet Timeline is released as RFC 2235 & FYI 32

La Fête de l'Internet, a country-wide Internet fest, is held in France 20-21 March

Companies flock to the Turkmenistan NIC in order to register their name under the .tm domain, the English abbreviation for trademark

Internet users get to be judges in a performance by 12 world champion ice skaters on 27 March, marking the first time a television sport show's outcome is determined by its viewers.

Network Solutions registers its 2 millionth domain on 4 May

Electronic postal stamps become a reality, with the US Postal Service allowing stamps to be purchased and downloaded for printing from the Web.

US$1M+ Domain Sales: Altavista.com (3.3M) to Compaq

Open source software comes of age

Technologies of the Year: E-Commerce, E-Auctions, Portals

Emerging Technologies: E-Trade, XML, Intrusion Detection

[HOBBES' INTERNET TIMELINE]

My move into domain names was to expose me to a space where the growing value of internet ventures rubbed up against governmental or private monopolies. I guess that these spaces are always going to be lucrative to players who understand them, but I came into the space as a neophyte and had to learn fast.

The two arenas in which I spent the last few years of the decade were the British domain name system and the global domain name system. While there were overlaps in terms of technology, there were almost none in terms of value and approach. These years were fast moving and exciting and, although I was only had a bit part, I participated in the domain name wars. I was a player.

The growth of the domain name system and the flow of money within it was a complex, international multi-dimensional business that continues to this day. The essence of it was that every use of the internet needed an address. A system had been created that put a human readable name on top of the long numeric addresses that computers could read. These name addresses were useful but in the early days considered fairly valueless because making one just involved making an entry in a database and demand was very low. In the US the job of doling them out was subsidised by the government and was given in the early nineties to a small consultancy called Network Solutions. They were paid a few million dollars a year to handle the process, and when we started to register names for ourselves and our clients, the process involved sending an email template as a request, which was then accepted or denied. The domain names ending in .com, .net and .org were all run by Network Solutions. There was literally a rule in the early days that you could only have one domain name and asking for more than one often resulted in a refusal.

We did understand the potential fun to be had from owning domain names as soon as we started building web sites, but we didn't see them as valuable. As they were free, we would sometimes come back from the pub and fire off dozens of requests for interesting names. As hardy any had been registered in the early days, almost anything could be had, but we were trying to be funny. One Xmas we registered as string of Christmas related names: babyjesus.com, rudolftherednosereindeer.com and many more. They were free and they were interesting, there was no more to it than that.

From the beginning of my time in the domain name industry, the monster in the room was a company called Network Solutions. They had managed to acquire control over the .com, .net and .org domains and had subsequently imposed a registration fee of $100 for each registration. This outrageous imposition almost brought down the nascent industry overnight, but it made Network Solutions both hugely powerful and hugely wealthy as the number of domain registrations soared ever higher with the exploding expansion of the commercial internet. As the world saw the huge fortunes being made by Internet startups there was a rush to join in. We were no longer alone in our world, we were being rushed from all directions, only now I felt that we had a product to sell the new arrivals. They all wanted a domain name and we had the best brand in the market - for the time being.

As the domain name industry started to grow it became clear that I was at the centre of a new thing that I'd almost invented, but that there were a lot of people who had different ideas about how it should proceed. In the early days both Network Solutions and the UK authorities imposed restrictions on what domain names could be registered and how many anyone could have.

In the UK the situation was trickier and ill. The right to issue domains was overseen, for arcane historic reasons, by an academic called Willie Black, but the actual process of issuing names was managed via a mailing list called, The Naming List. It was run and populated by the bigger ISPs, including British Telecom, Pipex and several others, who called themselves the Naming Committee. All of whom were determined to keep this process to themselves. However, someone told me that I was allowed to join the list as an observer, which I did. I was soon watching the process in astonishment.

To register a name, it was emailed to the mailing list. If nobody objected, it was passed and entered into the DNS. After this it could be used. There had never been much volume on this list, which was just as well because it was clearly going to break down in short order.

There were also some regulations around the registration of names in the UK, the main one being that you could only register the precise company name that you had or, as a loophole, the name you 'traded under'. As soon as they let my company join in the registration process I was determined to break it. I took the view that domain names were my business and there was no real reason to restrict what could be registered. I was acting on behalf of my clients and my future clients, but it was crucial for the continued success of NetNames.

My plan for breaking the Naming Committee's system was simple - we put in applications to register a range of sporting names: football.co.uk, rugby.co.uk, cricket.co.uk As anticipated, they were rejected. We appealed, saying they were names we were 'trading as'. We were asked to prove this, and in response we asked for the definition of trading as. There was no answer to this, we had found a major loophole and opened the floodgates.

After this, Dr Black decided to take control of the issuing of names by forming a non-profit company called Nominet. He tried to keep me off the board, but a few months later when the first board was elected by the new members I was elected. I served as a board member of Nominet until 2000.

I never much believed that the Internet was a space without rules, but I did come to believe that the domain name system could float free from the earth.

At the same time as I was building what I thought was a world leading company I had another problem, the sort of problem that had dogged my life. I couldn't get anyone to take me seriously. Not only was it hard to get the attention of the bigger companies that I wanted to partner with, but I started to feel that there were deals going on in the background that I never knew about. Although I clearly didn't, I felt I had some right to be considered as I had more or less invented this industry that was now growing rapidly. I think this was more another manifestation of my lifelong problem, my lack of self-esteem and my attention deficit, but it was starting to bother me.

I went to Japan for meeting of the CORE group. We were trying to work out an agreement that would take some of the unfettered power back from Network Solution in the domain name world. CORE was well ahead of its time but for a short period we thought we could change the world. In Japan many people from the industry met and at the end we elected someone to lead the organisation. I stood in this election and even produced a manifesto of sorts, a handout that set out my approach to the next phase of our project. I was beaten by a guy who had a business selling hair conditioners and who had never really said anything about how he would manage the group. I was upset and although CORE fell apart a short while later, it showed me that I didn't count for much in the business.

My American colleague, Anthony Van Couvering, who was the part owner and CEO of NetNames USA, took his pursuit of the Tuvalu domain to extreme lengths. He later recounted a tale of domain name exploration the likes of which I never heard again. Invited to visit the low-lying country to discuss the domain, he flew out to New Zealand where he met his contact. They flew on to a largeish island where this contact had a car waiting. This took them to the opposite end of the island. The Tuvaluan motioned to Anthony to climb into a small plane, took the controls and, without much ado, took off into the Pacific sky.

'We flew out over empty sea. After a while the sky darkened. I couldn't see any land and I began to get a feeling of extreme nervousness. We flew on into the setting sun and just as I was thinking we were done for the pilot circled a couple of times and swiftly landed the plane on a tiny strip of half-submerged land which had appeared out of the darkness.'

This was Tuvalu, the fabled owner of .tv, a domain akin to El Dorado in the lore of the domainers. Unfortunately, it was never to be ours as organisations with far deeper pockets soon entered the race and we were comprehensively outgunned. But many of the other unregarded domains briefly entered our registry.

We went to Washington to meet again about domain names and to discuss how to break the Network Solutions monopoly. We stayed at the Army and Navy Club which one of our members was part of. It was a surreal weekend. On the streets anti-abortion marchers marched and in the media Bill Clinton struggled against impeachment.

During the weekend an emissary brought a plan. Jon Postel, the sandal wearing bearded god-guru of domain names, was offering a solution, to take control of the A server that Network Solutions had in their tight grip. If we agreed to create new top-level domains according to his plan he would seize control of the server and empower us.

We agreed and Postel later hatched a cunning technical plan. He sent instructions to the managers of all the other servers, the B, C, D etc. down to J servers which normally replicated the A servers, acting as backups. These computers were mostly in university departments around the world and their owners were more beholden to Postel than to Network Solutions. He was one of theirs. The plan went ahead but late at night one of the recipients, not understanding the instructions, asked the hostmaster at the A server for clarification and thus tipped off Network Solutions to what plans were afoot. Their contact in government was abroad, travelling in Egypt with the President, but an urgent message was got to her and in return she contacted Postel immediately.

'You must reverse this process, immediately. Do you understand me?'

Postel was no stranger to the power of government. Despite affecting hippy ways and garb, he had spent decades in the pay of the military-industrial complex, the funded his work on domain names an internet protocol management. He was their boy and he caved.

The plan was finished and Network Solutions emerged as master of all they surveyed. They had won the domain name wars.

NETWORK SOLUTIONS SHARES SURGE 30 PERCENT IN IPO

September 27, 1997

Shares of Network Solutions Inc., the Herndon firm that has much envied exclusive rights to assign most Internet addresses, were offered to the public for the first time yesterday morning and surged almost 30 percent from the $18 opening price by day's end.

The quick rise, analysts said, was due to investors' confidence that the company will be able to thrive even if other firms are allowed to register addresses when Network Solutions' exclusive agreement with the National Science Foundation expires next year.

"It was an excellent showing," said Ken Fleming, an analyst with Renaissance Capital Corp., a Greenwich, Conn., firm that tracks initial public offerings, or IPOs. "It's a name that a lot of investors who know about the Internet recognize."

The offering also was aided by a recent run-up in other Internet stocks, analysts said. In the last two weeks, for example, share prices have jumped 35 percent for Internet bookseller Amazon.com Inc., 24 percent for Internet search firm Excite Inc. and 33 percent for online auctioneer Onsale Inc. Amazon.com shares, which closed at $50 yesterday, were initially offered to the public for $18 in May.

We looked at each country in the world to see whether it was possible to register a domain name and soon realised that this was a potential source of a new business, running the actual registries. One thing that surprised us was that a lot of countries didn't have their top level domain registered. There was no way to register a domain name in those countries because there was no initial registration, no entry of their domain into the system. We discovered that it was fairly simple to get these missing countries registered, and for a time we looked for partners to help us set up these new domains. NetNames became the largest country level registry in the world.

For obvious commercial reasons, some top level domains were more interesting than others. We ran down the list, wondering what alternative use could be made of these two letter combinations. Useful combinations included Tuvalu's .tv, Armenia's

.am, Moldova's .md and Micronesia's .fm and Libya's .ly. Top of our list came .tv but a close second was Turkmenistan's .tm, and it looked a lot easier to get hold of.

We set up and run the Libyan Top Level Domain, .ly and it caused us no end of problems. Libya was under American sanctions at the time and a feisty lawmaker, Representative for Mississippi, Charles "Chip" Pickering – keen footballer, farmer, and chairman of the US House Science Committee — decided to make something of it. Preposterously, his committee was considering legislation banning non-Americans from registering .com addresses (and also his horror at the idea of passing control of domain name admin to a bunch of foreign Swiss guys).

The committee suddenly became very concerned that Net-Names had been going around actually aiding and abetting Libya by running its .ly domain in direct contravention to the USA's foreign policy. As he wanted to make an example of someone, he aimed his fire at Anthony in the New York office. Libya was actually run out of London, and nothing more came of being denounced in the House.

We ran other top-level domains as well, but none of them got us into trouble, except perhaps Afghanistan. After I had sold NetNames to a company called Netbenefit and the US had invaded Afghanistan following 9/11, I got a panicked call from the CEO, Jonathan Robinson.

'What do you know about the Afghan domain?' he demanded. I didn't think I knew anything about it. I didn't even remember that we used to run it. It turned out that someone had looked up who ran the Afghan NIC and, finding NetNames listed, promptly hacked Netbenefit, who were the parent company. They left pro-US anti-Taliban graffiti all over poor old Net-benefit's site. This was the only episode of political vandalism that I was ever involved in, and it made me laugh despite being driven by a very serious event.

We thought we could launch a Trademark registration service using the extension .tm. At the time, the domain name wars were raging. The domain name community was eager to launch new TLDs. .com was sewn up as a monopoly by Network Solutions, who had launched a huge floatation on the strength of it. We felt that there was room in this game for the rest of us. And the game was attracting more and more hungry players.

While waiting and working and fighting for more top level domains, we decided to go out and acquire some that already existed, that could not be stopped by Network Solutions.

We found a partner in Turkmenistan, Batyr Karryev. I don't recall how we found him. He worked at a bank in Ashgabat and had a rudimentary internet connection. At least, he could send us the occasional email. We agreed terms: a split of revenues from .tm registrations would go to him. We would register local Turkmeni names for free and we would run the nic ourselves from London. We felt quite happy with the deal, and in May 1998 we launched .tm as a Trademark domain for the Internet.

Was this outrageous? In many ways, yes. At the time it didn't seem so strange. We knew we were in a fight for survival, as others poured into the business we had pioneered. We garnered a lot of press coverage, not all of it positive. The Times in London covered us:

Internet gets its Trademark thanks to London company

By Chris Ayres

The trademark symbol is coming to the Internet thanks to a bizarre alliance between a British company and the former Soviet Republic of Turkmenistan.

NetNames, a tiny London business, has struck a profit-sharing deal with the Government of Turkmenistan to sell companies the right to end their Internet addresses with the suffix ".TM" Although the ".TM" suffix carries no legal weight, since Monday, contracts for it have been sold to more than 1,000 companies, including Warner Brothers and Esso, for $50 (£30) a year.

The scheme is possible because the US authorities have allocated all countries with domain names -rather like international postcodes -- which tell computers in which parts of the world to find Internet sites. The British domain name is ".UK" -- Turkmenistan is ".TM".

However, most large companies are loath to use national domain names and have instead paid huge premiums to register under the only two international names of ".COM" or ".ORG". Now that nearly all brands in all languages have been registered under ".COM" and ".ORG" a row has erupted over the need for more international names, an over who should be in charge of creating them. At present, the US authorities have complete control. NetNames says that it can offer a short-term solution with the name ".TM".

"There is no such thing as an Internet trademark," says Ivan Pope, chief executive. "But everyone recognises the meaning of .TM"

Soon after a successful launch, we ran into difficulties. Karryev, our local contact, started to play up. He claimed that there were problems with the contract. I felt that he was being got at by people who were jealous of our launch and who wanted to take .tm for themselves. We fought a short battle to keep the domain live, but froze the nic later that year, with existing domains still working but no new entries being made. We were asked to go to Turkmenistan to negotiate over the contract, but I had visions of men in sheepskins and Kalashnikovs taking me hostage. I decided to let it go. There were problems with the small tld's, as Wired recognised.

Soon after, the .tm registry became functional again. It was still registered to NetNames, still registered at our old address and still listing Karryev as our Turkmeni contact. The one thing that had changed was that it was run by the very person who seemed to be manoeuvring against us in 1998. This was truly the wild west of the Internet.

17

Last Days of the New World

1999

Internet access becomes available to the Saudi Arabian (.sa) public in January

vBNS sets up an OC48 link between CalREN South and North using Juniper M40 routers

IBM becomes the first Corporate partner to be approved for Internet2 access

European Parliament proposes banning the caching of Web pages by ISPs

The Internet Fiesta kicks off in March across Europe, building on the success of La Fête de l'Internet held in 1998

US State Court rules that domain names are property that may be garnished

A forged Web page made to look like a Bloomberg financial news story raised shares of a small technology company by 31% on 7 April.

ICANN announces the five testbed registrars for the competitive Shared Registry System

SETI Home launches on 17 May and within four weeks its distributed Internet clients provide more computing power than the most powerful supercomputer of its time (:par:)

First large-scale Cyberwar takes place simultaneously with the war in Serbia/Kosovo

Abilene, the Internet2 network, reaches across the Atlantic and connects to NORDUnet and SURFnet

The Web becomes the focal point of British politics as a list of MI6 agents is released on a UK Web site. Though forced to remove the list from the site, it was too late as the list had already been replicated across the Net. (15 May)

Somalia gets its first ISP - Olympic Computer (Sep)

Free computers are all the rage (as long as you sign a long term contract for Net service)

US$1M+ Domain Sales: business.com (7.5M on 30 Nov), Wine.com (2.9M), Autos.com (2.2M), WallStreet.com (1M in Apr)

Technologies of the Year: E-Trade, Online Banking, MP3

Emerging Technologies: Net-Cell Phones, Thin Computing, Embedded Computing

Viruses of the Year: Melissa (March), ExploreZip (June)

[HOBBES' INTERNET TIMELINE]

Towards the end of the millennium, I went to California again to visit my friend and investor, Keith Teare, at his new offices and get his view of where my company, NetNames, should head. I was there for some R&R and some serious research.

The Internet was becoming mainstream and the stock markets, led by the quaintly named National Association of Securities Dealers Automated Quotations index (Nasdaq) in New York, couldn't get enough .com stocks. We had taken to watching the market fluctuations like transfixed meerkats.

The year before I had attempted to sell my business to a company called Network Solutions, a process that would have made me rich beyond dreams of avarice but which had, in the end, fallen apart badly. I had the feeling that I owed Keith something, that I had fluffed the situation. To some degree I also felt that it had maybe been Keith's over helpful lawyers and their astronomical pricing input that had scuppered a deal and that maybe he could help me find a new route to a payoff. His startup, Realnames, seemed to be doing very well. They had moved offices into a vast new block in a strange part of the valley.

His company had been born on a kitchen table in Marylebone while he was still living in London. He had shown me some business plans that he was mulling over, one of which was called Go Corporation. It was similar to things I was doing and was obviously born out of my experience with domain names. He had a plan to create a new addressing system from scratch and then get everyone to buy into it. I didn't take it too seriously at first, as the barriers to success seemed huge. If there was going to be a new system, thought, it was going to have to be attacked from a different place. Keith thought he had an angle.

On moving to America, he moved with his wife, Gene, into a bungalow just off the legendary Sand Hill Road, where the venture capitalists hung out. He never did anything by half, he had an almost mystical way of getting to the heart of a project. Venture capitalists loved him and he was a long way now from the Revolutionary Communist Party, where he had once sat on the central committee. He had gone from revolutionary communist to revolutionary capitalist almost without blinking, I thought. The house was typically Californian. It had a swimming pool in the backyard, but there was never anyone in it. Keith and Gene were tasting wines and noting their responses in a small notebook like good Californian autodidacts.

I hired my usual sporty American car that drove like a boat and took it down to their house. We seldom ate in. They had adopted the American way of eating out all the time. One lunchtime we went to eat in a large vogueish pizza joint near the university. When we arrived, there was a certain buzz in the place. 'Bill has just been in' they said. That was Bill Gates, at that point absolutely the master of the universe.

Keith's company was properly funded. They had been round the houses. I had seen each office they took. A small, homely space in a mall first. By the time I came back to see how they were getting on, they had moved on to an anonymous space within a defence contractor style all American office block. I visited just after they moved in, an empty carpeted shell with acres of space. The next time I saw it, it was full of cubicles. Keith had recruited well and he was well connected. He raised another round and took a huge space in an upcoming part of the valley. A new block, a huge, curved floor with views over the freeway. When I arrived Realnames was moving in. The space had been designed by a UK architect, all industrial groove, podlike meeting rooms, long working benches, reception and more free food in the huge kitchens than you would find in the canteen of a UK company. I hung out for a few days. The vibe was brilliant. It was a company in full flood. Keith was the man. The plan that I had read on his kitchen table back in London three years before had transformed into this huge company. He had hired well. Everyone was on board, though it was almost impossible to understand who was doing what. Down one end of the space were salespeople. Up another end, the technical staff. In the middle, management, lawyers, directors, dreamers.

The company was properly funded. In the scheme of things, it had the money to get up and go. Keith was an evangelist and a believer. He had brought Microsoft and Netscape to the table and convinced them that they should deal, but it wasn't selling anything. No-one understood its product. The problem, clear to me, was that if it worked, Microsoft would want to own the product. And Microsoft held the trumps over the entire company.

Realnames were moving into the sky. Many of the people he had talked to over the last couple of years were now inside the company, and the company was humming. It was in the blue sky with a long way to fall.

We commissioned a Russian company to build us a name registration management system from scratch during our entanglement with the US company of my friend, Alan Sullivan. I had been obsessed with this idea from day one and had repeatedly tried to get it built, but somehow we never got anywhere near it. Maybe I was just too ambitious.

When Alan suggested that he would manage the project and we would subcontract to these genius Russians, I thought we were saved. We made the deal and a while later their advance team arrived in our London office to find out what we did and how we did it. They used a very specific coding system that involved them drawing lots of nice charts of our procedures that would then be converted into the code by the team back in Moscow.

The couple who came to London got on well with us but didn't seem to have the faintest idea of what we were doing. I had assumed that they would talk to us and find out what we did, what we wanted to do and what we didn't want to do. Then they would go and build an all singing all dancing product, but it seemed that what we understood instinctively didn't translate very well into the Russian system.

While this was going on, I would escape by going to the New York office. However, it wasn't much better over there. Since we had defenestrated the US founder that office had got weirder on a monthly basis. I had absolutely no idea what was really going on. I had managed to plant my own man, an Australian, in the finance role. I had flown out and spent a few weeks practically living in the office. After a month I decided that this was no way to have a life, let alone a family. I started to look for someone to run the US office. I knew this was a gamble, as there would be no-one to oversee whoever I hired. However, I had to do it. I pulled one of the many over willing and expensive New York recruitment agencies and we got to work.

In Autumn a magazine, New Media Creative, launched. Paul Murphy, the editor, was a friend and he asked me to write a monthly column. I was billed as the 'been-there-done-that man'. My first column was titled 'Niche work if you can get it'. I offered four (extremely) tongue in cheek ways to get rich at the start of the next millennium, including starting a web site called Ifancyashag.com, something that later came very much to be.

Well, someone has to do it. It doesn't have to be crude or rude. No dirty pictures. But wouldn't it be nice if there was a site where you could let the world know that what you most wanted at this precise moment was a shag? Add in your location co-ordinates, facilities available ("I'm in Trafalgar Square/I'm ensconced in Suite 3234 of the Ri   ") and away you go. Regulars could have their own private "rooms" with details of when they are most likely to fancy a shag, ie. after six pints of lager on a Friday night. Taking a cue from eBay again, you could offer "peer judgement", by which new users of the service could take account of comments and grades from previous shaggers.

One morning in his office Keith Teare told me that someone we both knew, Tom Barrett, had been made redundant. Barrett worked for Thompson and Thompson, the big boys of intellectual property, and had made a name for himself as a mover and shaker of domain name registration.

I had met Tom a couple of years earlier in London. He had come to see me to tell me about Thompson and Thompson's domain name project which was growing out of their established Compumark service. I felt intimidated, though I was happy to have a contact at the heart of their project. I felt that I was positioned to do a deal, if a deal was to be done. But Tom was a strange character, a Bostonian working class boy with a slight speech impediment, he always seemed very sure of himself, but didn't quite make sense. I put this down to his background in large American corporations. It wasn't unusual for Americans to make me feel uncomfortable. I had yet to learn that this generally happened in inverse proportion to their effectiveness. I think the US corporate culture made people either relax and swing with the world or close down and build barriers to being understood. To be understood was to be exposed. In a big outfit, people could spend years evading detection and disposal. Tom had perfected the art, but even he could not blend in forever. There were reasons for his redundancy, but at the time I was too excited by the thought of hiring a real CEO to pay them any heed.

When I heard that Thompson & Thompson had closed down Tom's project and he was unemployed my response was, 'idiots'. I was confident that we were unchallengeable on the domain name front and I assumed Thompson and Thompson just didn't get it. We did. Keith said, 'Get over to Boston and hire him. You've got your CEO'. So, I rang him up and arranged to meet up.

I flew into Boston a couple of days later. Again, I felt very exposed. I was not the best numbers man around. In fact, I was probably the worst numbers man around. I didn't know whether this would be an issue. I could carry most people on my enthusiasm alone, and anyone with a vision generally came along for the ride. But sometimes a discussion on the numbers would be called for, and I would be found lacking. I had never learnt balance sheets and had no-one in the company who could deliver for me the understanding and analysis that I needed.

I went to meet Tom at his old office. I didn't really think he would take a job with NetNames, but I wanted to position myself and I wanted to impress Keith.

The offices were a depressing sight. Standard US type accommodation, it had obviously been emptied out in a hurry. Boston was a world away from California and Silicon Valley, even from New York and its nascent Silicon Alley. It seemed slow and detached, small and unworldly. Of course, it had its own .com startups, every city in the world now had its startups, and every city in the world had or wanted its version of Silicon Valley. Each of the cities claiming to be natural venues for the .com boom had its local cliques, its local successes and its local colour. The bubble was moving into top gear and the world had been converted. The internet meme had been joined by an instant wealth meme. Everyone knew of the vast amounts of cash generated by early internet entrepreneurs. Even those who didn't believe it had decided that the internet changed the rules of everything, including how to make money, It had become common to be offered business plans inappropriately as in meetings with your lawyer or bank manager. They would surreptitiously pull a sheaf of papers out of their pocket and ask shyly if you would have a look at it. Everyone had a plan, everyone wanted to get rich.

We sat in a windowless corner office and bandied industry chat. Tom brought his second in command along to the meeting and I assumed they would come as a pair. However, it soon became apparent that Tom was being ditched. I assumed he would be lining up jobs, but he seemed indifferent to the industry. He was very keen on NetNames though. He waved a huge strategy document under my nose. I was impressed and thought he would just bring it along to NetNames and implement it. I never asked him why T&T had fired him and closed down his department. It never occurred to me to ask what he was doing or how he intended to work when he came on board.

After two days, we agreed that Tom was going to come and be the CEO of NetNames International and that I would step up to the role of Chair. I was demob happy. It suddenly seemed that I had a way out, a way to unload the company, or at least stop being totally responsible for it twenty-four hours a day. I reckoned without the incompetence of Tom and the reaction of my team back in London. There was also the small matter of the New York office. Tom was a Bostonian through and through. He was the twelfth son of a Bostonian, he had a wife and a growing brood of kids in Boston and by golly, he wasn't going to move to New York. I left the geography hanging, reasoning that as CEO he would make the right decision. I wasn't even sure I had.

I flew down to Virginia to see Alan Sullivan, whose company we were supposed to be merging with. I was becoming unsure as to what we were merging with and I couldn't see the deal concluding, but I also didn't want to call it off myself. I liked Alan and his wife and I liked going to visit him. I decided to leave a decision on the merger to Tom as his first test.

There were issues at NetNames in London. Staff numbers had grown to around twenty in the London office and maybe fifteen in New York. London ran quite well, though I had no idea what Phil was doing with the accounts. A lot of money flowed in at one end, but there never seemed to be any left at the other end. I hadn't come to grips with finances. Presented with profit and loss or cash flow, it was like being back at school in the chemistry lab with chemistry equations and a grumpy teacher.

The business was being run by Cath and Rob, who between them could be relied upon to keep everyone in the office and to turn up, at least one of them each day. The rest of the office staff were settled and on the whole knew what they were doing. Our systems needed a lot of attention, but in the full flow of business it just wasn't going to get it -- that's what the Russians were for. In the meantime, we staggered on with the database that had been written for us years previously, something that did what we wanted, but didn't really do it the way we wanted.

I was getting jumpy. My desire to start an incubator and do properly what I had been doing for the last seven years, helping businesses get started, was in danger of getting swept away in the rush. If everybody and their uncle could launch and float an internet company, then what chance did mine have. I had been negotiating the sale of NetNames for several months and was still bogged down in detail, let alone the Year2000 bug audits.

The Financial Times had become the house journal of the bubble. I had never been able to read it before. It seemed turgid and obscure, obsessed with British engineering firms and leveraged buyouts. Suddenly every page was do ed with exciting internet deals that both inspired and appalled me.

Everyone was so scared of the Y2K bug that they drove themselves into a frenzy. That this was largely created by the forces of consultancy never seemed to cross anyone's mind. My deal was coming towards its conclusion and the grind of accountants and lawyers was almost complete, but Y2K had created one of the most insuperable obstacles. Our little string and sealing wax software system was never going to withstand their professional probing or to reassure them. A problem was that the valuations of our companies had grown so large, our ambitions to join the main stock market so traditional, that a different set of assumptions came into play. In the end I simply stopped paying attention and let things get handled by the tech guys, who were excellent at creating diversionary bullshit.

In the middle of 1999, I was invited to lunch by Keith Young, patriarch of the Whitfield St internet generation. He had schlepped his companies around the market, gaining a reputation as a man who dealt. And you had to hand something to him, he had been there to invest in Keith's first company, Easynet, when they were young. He had had his payoff from that gamble, though he was unhappy that he had dumped his shares for pennies before the bubble came and took them into the pounds. I never had any idea of how rich he was, but he was certainly far richer than me. I was trying to buy my flat in Camden, he lived in a townhouse in Chelsea.

I rather liked him. He was considered unclean by some in that he wasn't obvious .com boomer. He was older and had independent wealth from a previous life in reprographics. Rumour held that his company brought him a million pounds a year in profit.

The invite was not unexpected. He had just taken his copycat company, Netbenefit, public on the AIM market and it had a decent share price. This gave them power and made it harder for us to get listed, even if we could find someone to believe in us. An approach was certain, as we had the brand recognition and growth that they were having trouble reaching.

He asked me whether I would like to have lunch with him and booked us into a place in Mayfair. When I arrived, I knew at once that this was a real deal. The restaurant was a suitably high-class establishment. I'm no judge of restaurants above a certain level, and I certainly didn't know what's in and what's out, but this place just spoke the business. The clincher was the amuse bouche. A small cup of frothy light soup with a quail's egg in it arrived before we'd ordered anything. It certainly amused my mouth, and the discussion got off to a good start.

It must have been about the fourth time I'd sat and discussed selling my company with a solicitous man in a suit. It was probably the first time that I believed, really believed, that it could be done. My dalliance with Virtual Internet was public knowledge, as was its ending. Since going round the houses a year earlier, the Netbenefit CEO had avoided me like the plague.

There were issues at my company. Staff had grown to around twenty in the London office and maybe fifteen in New York. London ran quite well, though I had no idea what Phil was doing with the accounts. A lot of money flowed in at one end, but there never seemed to be any left at the other. I still hadn't come to grips with accounts. Presented with profit and loss or cash flow, it was like being back at school in the chemistry lab with chemistry equations. I only had a vague grasp of how we were doing.

The business was being run day to day by Cath and Rob, who between them could be relied upon to keep everyone in the office and to turn up, at least one of them, each day. The rest of the office staff were settled and on the whole knew what they were doing. Our systems needed a lot of attention, but in the full flow of growth they just weren't going to get it. We staggered on with the database that had been written for us a couple of years previously, something that did what we wanted, but didn't really do it the way we wanted.

Keith Young offered me a good deal. He wanted to merge Net-Names with his existing listed company, Netbenefit which was itself the result of the merger of two companies. He offered me a third of the combined companies and I took it. I was bored and worn out. I knew I was at the limit of my ability to manage this thing. More, I believed that together and with a listing we could do great things. I imagined us growing and growing, doing mergers and acquisitions deals and becoming a billion-dollar company. Of course, I would have little role in this new company. I would be on the board but have no job.

I took the deal. It was worth, at the start, six million pounds, to be paid mostly in shares in the new company. There was an interesting aspect to what they were doing: they wanted to move the new company to the main London stock market at the same time as making the merger. As I soon came to realise, this meant we were playing for higher stakes and were in a more serious game. Luckily I didn't have to do much of the real work, I just had to play along.

From the moment the heads of agreement was signed things moved into a different gear. Top end accountants, Deloittes, and lawyers and advisors were introduced to the mix. They started to crawl all over NetNames' books and soon revealed some alarming problems. We were running out of money.

As the year progressed and the deal ground slowly onwards, the internet markets went into hyperdrive. More and more companies were going public and around the world a huge .com boom was being built with valuations soaring into the stratosphere. Even our little deal became richer and richer. After a while this started to bother the other side.

They started to try and put pressure on me to reduce the value of the deal and I spent a considerable amount of time fending them off while at the same time fighting to keep my own company solvent. The months ticked by in a succession of endless meetings with the lawyers and the accountants in smart London offices while in my office we struggled to keep our heads above water. The accountants audited us and didn't like what they found. They attempted to audit our software and found it was held together with string and sticky tape. We carried on selling a lot of domain names during this period but I could see the industry was changing and American startups made inroads into our business.

On top of all the difficulties we found ourselves in, the millennium was fast approaching and with it a global fear of what was known as the Y2K bug which theoretically might, on the stroke of midnight on the last day of the year, cause all sorts of businesses to collapse. Without going into details of why this might have been, a large industry of consultants grew up, happy to milk the situation. As we were intending to move to the full London stock market around the time of the millennium they decided that we had too be squeaky clean on the technology front. The problem was, we had built our systems on the cheap over a few years with no documentation.

Nobody was happy and the work stretched on and on. I started to wonder if it would ever complete.

The night of the new millennium caused a global stomach cramp. In London a River of Fire was supposed to run up the Thames, but what everyone really wanted was to hear of planes dropping out of the sky, nuclear power stations blowing up and medical operations coming to a standstill mid incision. We were so primed that it seemed inconceivable that this would not, at some level, come true. In the end nothing happened. Nothing. The world continued to spin on its axis. All the Y2K spend was quietly put aside and forgotten and in London we got on with our deal.

The .com boom had infected all spheres of activity. The stock market had roared off into space. My daughter was born on the second of February, an auspicious date: the first for almost a thousand years with no odd numbers in it. Failing to read the signs, and fearing family entrapment, I started a new company, it's what I did. I'd proved I could do it, although looking back I never had any idea of what I'd done. I didn't know about attention deficit or creative vision, about epiphany, I just was having the time of my life. It all had to end in tears.

I had made a bet I couldn't really afford on a process that I didn't really understand and that I certainly wasn't in control of. Across London, across the western world, across the markets of the entire world, others were doing the same thing. The man I shared my office with, Chris Moss, was doing it. He had come. up with the name Orange for the eponymous phone company. He was famous in his world. Now he wanted to mortgage his house, to raise money to get his startup to the starting gate. He didn't want to build a business, no one wanted to build a business any more. They wanted a niche, to occupy a niche. To have a company to trade, to deal, to place on the table. They wanted to be an operator, to live. To have an internet company in play at that time was very bliss. And despite the fact that I had been building internet companies since 1993, I realised I didn't have anything in play. I was as much a startup as everyone else. Thing was, everyone was doing the same thing.

The build up to the new year became a frenzy as everyone jumped onto the speeding waggon, convinced of major drama. Stories circulated, based on the Y2K bug, that aeroplanes would fall out of the sky, hospitals would cease to function and all money would become valueless. For this reason, surgeons postponed operations, travellers postponed flights (or jumped on board, relishing the sudden drop in fares) and the price of Krugerrands soared as hoarders prepared for the apocalypse.

18

Decline and Fall

2000

The US timekeeper (USNO) and a few other time services around the world report the new year as 19100 on 1 Jan

A massive denial of service attack is launched against major web sites, including Yahoo, Amazon, and eBay in early February

Web size estimates by NEC-RI and Inktomi surpass 1 billion indexable pages

ICANN selects new TLDs: .aero, .biz, .coop, .info, .museum, .name, .pro (16 Nov)

After months of legal proceedings, the French court rules Yahoo! must block French users from accessing hate memorabilia in its auction site (Nov). Given its inability to provide such a block on the Internet, Yahoo! removes those auctions entirely (Jan 2001). The case is eventually thrown out (Feb 2003).

Technologies of the Year: ASP, Napster

Emerging Technologies: Wireless devices, IPv6

Viruses of the Year: Love Letter(May)

Lawsuits of the Year: Napster, DeCSS

[HOBBES' INTERNET TIMELINE]

The Millennium, so anticipated, so worked towards, so feared, was quickly lost in history. The new world we imagined so fondly never really arrived but the dangers we told ourselves about never transpired either. Instead we quickly built ourselves a whole new set of problems, exacerbated by the existence of this communications platform that I loved. It was only twelve years since I had come across the it in the steampunk computer lab. The world was changing so much, but we had no idea what was coming next.

I watched all of this go past in a blur. I was selling my company, the deed was signed, the process engaged with. Somehow, nobody could make the deal happen without spending vast amounts of money. The accountants gathered, the lawyers clustered around us. Professional services came to the party.

On January 10th, America Online announced it was to merge with Time Warner in the largest merger ever. America Online had grown into a giant on the back of the Internet and had bought Netscape, the first of the new wave of successful Internet companies, in 1999 for $4.2 billion in stock. The merger was seen by many as a natural outcome of the new order. To others it looked like a step too far. Alan Greenspan started to raise interest rates aggressively.

On March 10th, the Nasdaq stock market index peaked at 5,048.

Failing to read the signs, and fearing the demands of my new babies, I planned a new company even before I had finished selling the old. I made a bet I couldn't afford on a process that I didn't understand and wasn't in control of.

Across London, across the western world, everyone was doing much the same. The seemingly endless wealth that was being generated from public flotations had sent everyone a bit crazy and they all wanted their own slice. Suddenly everyone was an entrepreneur, everyone had a startup, everyone had a plan — even those who were still in full time jobs. For a while I couldn't go anywhere without someone pulling an executive summary out of their pocket and asking me to have a look at it. Taxi drivers did it, old friends did it, waiters did it. Even my dentist had a plan.

I met and ended up sharing an office with a man, Chris Moss, who had come up with the name Orange for the mobile phone company. He had his own startup, of course, and was even more desperate to succeed than I was. He didn't really want to build a business, no-one wanted to do the hard work any more. They wanted to occupy a niche, to have a company to trade, to deal, to be at the table. To have an internet company at that time was very bliss but, despite the fact that I had just sold a very real company for a large amount of money, I also didn't have much to offer. Or, at least, nobody seemed to want to take me seriously. I had always told myself, had believed, that once I'd exited, once I'd built and sold a company, I would have a seat at the top table.

I thought I would be able to raise money for my next project, open doors and walk through. I was a believer and I thought I would soon have my own billion-pound company. It turned out not to be true though. I found out that I was as much a startup as anyone else — and my money was finite. I told Chris not to mortgage his house to save his business. I had borrowed a quarter of a million pounds against my shareholding and now found I had no way to pay it back.

On January 10th American Online announced a deal to merge with Time Warner in the largest merger ever. In retrospect it was a patently stupid move, but the markets saw it as further validation of their genius and shares continued to soar upwards, not recognising this was the real peak of the .com bubble. A few years later the deal would be described as 'the worst ever' and the CEOs who engineered it would be forced out. That day it had seemed more like a portent, a sign that we could all build billion-dollar conglomerates, and that was what I believed. I went into a deal to sell my company with my eyes open and a song in my heart, despite knowing almost nothing about how these things worked.

The next day, on January 11th, 2000, in the early hours of the morning, after months of haggling, procrastination and fear, I was called to a solicitor's office in Clerkenwell. My lawyer was there. He stood by the table in his expensive suit and gestured towards a long line of documents.

'Sign them all,' he said.

I moved along the row and signed everything that was there. When I had finished he shook my hand and smiled broadly. I'm sure he had never expected to reach this point.

'What happens next?' I asked.

'Go home and sleep, I'll sort out the shares,' he said.

In the morning my bank account contained an extra five hundred thousand pounds and my shares were worth thirty million.

I never saw any of the paperwork again but the deal was done. I had sold my company.

Two weeks later I phoned my lawyer.

'I haven't got my share certificate,' I said.

'I sent it to you,' he told me, laconically.

'How?'

'I put it in the post.'

'What sort of post?' I said.

'Just the ordinary post.'

He had put my share certificate in the post and thirty-five million pounds worth of shares had gone missing.

My daughter was born on the second of February 2000.

I now had two children, one born either side of the new era, something that put my family's historic caesura over the fifties versus the sixties into context. My daughter's birth date was considered auspicious, though it hadn't occurred to me, only when I saw it in the paper did I notice. It was the first date for almost a thousand years with no odd numbers in it. I had to think about that, counting backwards and then forwards in my head. Something like after 888 there were no more odd numbers. I couldn't be bothered to work it out in detail, to check whether I was right, I had a new baby to look after, and no job. Panic overtook me. I feared being left at home with the baby, being a house husband just as I had liberated myself to do whatever I wanted. But what did I want? I wanted to start new businesses. I wanted to savour the pleasure of genesis rather than the slog of management over time.

I called my new company Pregenesis. It means before the start of everything, I thought. I liked that, but nobody else did. It was an incubator, a briefly popular notion in which we would support a range of startup, fund them through the early days, bring teams in and watch them fly. Something like that. In retrospect it was world class stupid. I burned fast through my cash dowry from the sale, renting the expensive premises in Portman Square and letting myself hire a bunch of grifters who were happy to take my money and lard my dreams.

Desite my years of experience, I really had no idea what I was doing. I laid out grand plans for an incubator, a hothouse for startups. It was one of those things from that era, help new startups come to life and benefit from owning a part of them. A great idea, if you can create valuable startups. If you don't run out of money. If you understand how money works.

I never learnt how to raise money. I've never really done it. I've written a lot of business plans. Well, not really business plans, just literate outlines, clever one liners, collections of references and evidence. Nothing I've ever done has come anywhere close to raising actual money from actual investors. It's almost as if I have a clanging bell and red light on my head screaming, steer clear. I thought I had proved my point. I had created a business from scratch, stuck with it and made a decent exit. But the world was full of trained accountants and lawyers, financiers and business school graduates doing the same thing with bells on. They could write business plans, I couldn't. My purity of belief and my track record as a visionary amounted to nothing in this climate.

A prophet is not recognised in his own land — nor in any others.

My new team sat in a rented office on Portman Square, high above a glass atrium with glass lifts. Across the square was my club, Home House, previously the London base of the Home family, and pronounced 'Hume', though no-one did except me. It contained a listed Adams staircase, grand rooms, gloomy meeting rooms, subterranean gym and plunge pool and somewhere, hidden upstairs, bedrooms. A club for an era where everyone was a millionaire. It was ridiculously pompous but strangely anti-elitist and for a while let in without question almost anyone who knocked at the door, I would cross the square at lunchtime and eat a huge sandwich in the upstairs members rooms or drink at their huge comfy padded bar, savouring the untouchable luxury of it, aware of the fact that I was eating the most expensive sandwich in London. I would have used their gym, only it was somewhere in the lower depths and had such an arcane booking system that I never got to grips with. I would have used their internet connection, except they had not yet the internet installed. In the era of Only Connect, many places had not yet connected at all.

One day as I left the office, I was introduced to a smallish man in a grey suit. 'This is Charles' said Chris. 'Charles Dunstone'. Dunstone was the founder of Carphone Warehouse, successful surfer of the mobile phone wave. He had started out selling brick like mobiles from the back pages of magazines. He was about to float his company for a billion pounds. Dunstone was written about in the real press. He had transcended any shady beginnings, any time when he might not have known exactly what he was doing, what to do next. He had transcended fear and confusion, solitude and naivety. He was real. A real billion-pound businessman.

I always felt inadequate when I met people like this. Not that they had a clue what I was about, but I knew. I wasn't worth enough to talk to, though he was very polite and solicitous. I wasn't worth much because all my businesses were fake, startups or, worse, I had sold them to someone else. I wasn't a player. I didn't have anything to say, but if I had it would have been pointless. He was on another planet; he had a real company. I wasn't clubbable, though I was the largest shareholder of a real stock market company, I didn't exist.

We were trying to raise twelve, or ten, or eight or five million pounds for my new company. I had filled an office with bright people and they were eating my cash pile. Everything was eating my cash pile, but everyone just looked at my paper wealth and said, 'Well done' and 'You've already done it, you've made your millions. Now we have to make ours.' Everyone thought they could be multi-millionaires by the end of the year. I tried to tell them; in some parts of the world you can be whacked for ten dollars. There is no way you will be given millions of pounds. No way.

For myself, I believed that I had proved the point. I had been through the internet boom. No-one could touch me, I was golden. I had built and sold a company, and everyone that I met was lower down the food chain. I didn't carry a folded business plan in my suit pocket to brandish at unsuspecting bankers and lawyers. I didn't have to dream up strange me-too plans, ways to leverage, to niche, to change the paradigm. I had won. I could relax. Deep inside, I felt sick.

I ordered some Basse s' jelly babies from a startup called Urbanfetch. They were spending someone else's money faster than my team were spending mine. In fact, they were redistributing someone else's money to me. They were so keen to courier that they would deliver a bag of biscuits, chocolate, crisps with no delivery charge, no minimum order. We liked to take the piss, ordering jelly-babies for mid-afternoon. They came beautifully packaged. Even the couriers were beautifully packaged. We mocked them in their absence. Imagine, we said, millions of pounds on a courier company with a web site. It can't last. I felt happy to know that one of the people who had bought my company was heavily invested in Urbanfetch London. I wanted the reassurance that it could fail.

I sat in Portman Square, ate my subsidised jelly babies and waited. I bit off the heads, the legs, the arms, and swallowed the bodies.

On Friday the thirteenth of March 2000, my paper wealth hit a new high. My shares closed at seventeen pounds apiece, giving me a value of forty million, eight hundred thousand pounds. I went home to my son and my one-month-old daughter and said nothing. I felt sick. Everyone watched the monitors, day in day out. No-one worked. They wanted to see how rich I was, as if it made them richer. It was a good sport, check the price and shout down the office 'Up fifty pee' or 'Up five million'. At the other end of the office, Chris chatted to Richard Branson. I waited for an introduction.

The following Monday my wealth climbed to sixty million pounds exactly, then the market turned. By closing that day I had lost nine million pounds. The crash had begun.

A few weeks later I made most of my employees redundant and moved the company to an office at my friend's PR company. A few weeks after that the money finally ran out and we all left. The office became a ad empty place. I didn't know what to do with the equipment that we'd eagerly bought so recently. For years my children used colourful Apple computers and my desk drawer was filled with a lifetime supply of post it notes.

Entirely broke, I was persuaded to liquidate the remains of my new empire. All across London companies big and small were doing the same. The boom had run out of road. It almost seemed as if the Internet itself was finished. I turned the lights out in our office.

The dream was over for me. The first phase of the Internet was over. The first wave of big Internet companies were now facing extinction and many would go to the wall over the next year, although Amazon and eBay would survive and prosper. Pets.com, Webvan and Boo.com disappeared without trace, taking billions of investors dollars with them. Google was in its infancy, to small to be affected. There was no social media Facebook and Twitter were years away, as was the iPhone and all that followed from it. It would take many years before the Internet really got started again, and the next time around it would be very different. The Nasdaq market didn't reach the same high point for another fifteen years in 2015.

I wouldn't be there for the next phase. You can only do this once and I'd had enough. The following year, just before the disaster of 9/11 and the nightmare world it beckoned in, I moved out of London to the coast so my children could grow up quietly.